COMBAT MEDIC

An Australian's eyewitness account of the Kibeho Massacre

COMBAT MEDIC

An Australian's eyewitness account of the Kibeho Massacre

Terry Pickard

BIG SKY PUBLISHING

First published in 2008

Copyright © Terry Pickard 2008

Big Sky Publishing Pty Ltd
14 Rilatt Street
Wavell Heights, QLD, 4012
Australia
Phone: (61 2) 9918 2168
Fax: (61 2) 9918 2396
Email: info@bigskypublishing.com.au
Web: www.bigskypublishing.com.au

The National Library of Australia Cataloguing-in-Publication entry
Pickard, Terry, 1959
Combat Medic: an Australian's eyewitness account of the Kibeho Massacre
ISBN: 9780980325126
Pickard, Terry, 1959--United Nations--Peacekeeping forces--Rwanda.
Peacekeeping forces--Rwanda. Rwanda--Civil War, 1994--Personal narratives, Australian--Rwanda--Civil War, 1994--Atrocities.
967.5710431092

Copy Editor Alastair Mival
Proofreading and edit by Denny Neave, Sharon Evans and Anna Kassulke
Cover and layout design by Think Productions
Typesetting by Think Productions
Cover Photography courtesy Department of Defence and Army Newspaper
Printed in Australia by PMP Print Pty Ltd

For all those who have suffered PTSD.

For my wife Nicole who endures my PTSD.

For Dr Malcolm Foxcroft who treats my PTSD.

For the people of Rwanda who suffered so terribly.

For the Royal Australian Medical Corps.

Contents

Acknowledgments

I would like to acknowledge the following people who have been instrumental in the writing and publishing of this book.

Without help from Dr Malcolm Folcroft, MBBS, FRANZCP, I would not have been able to tell any of my story. Not only did he give me the strength to live with post-traumatic stress disorder, he also gave me the strength to face my demons and get them on paper.

Ross Coulthart from the Channel Nine *Sunday* programme, who first brought the story of the forgotten soldiers who served in Rwanda during the Kibeho Massacre to the public's attention. Ross has continually provided me with advice and encouraged me to complete this book.

I would like to thank George Gittoes (www.gittoes.com) for permission to use many of the photos that appear in this book.

My wife, Nicole, who gave me all the time and support I needed to sit and write. She has also been my greatest and best critic.

Denny Neave and his team at Big Sky Publishing, who read my draft and then went all out to make the book a success.

My brother, Ken, who has pulled me out of some of the worst times I have ever had.

My best mate, Nico, he knows why.

Finally, I would like to thank the 32 finest Australian soldiers who held fast on those terrible days between 18th and 22nd April, 1995 in Kibeho, Rwanda. That was the most horrific and terrifying time which culminated in the massacre. If they had not held fast, I know none of us would be alive to tell the story. I am proud to be one of you.

Introduction

April 22, 1995

The rain intensified as it swept across the valley to our front. All around us the shooting died away. When we were sure it was safe enough to stand up we started moving away from our position. Five of us had spent the past couple of hours crouched behind the knee-high sandbag wall. The bunker felt pathetically small, but somehow it protected all of us from the Rwandan Patriotic Army's (RPA) ferocious incoming fire. Even though they were not firing at us directly, a lot of their rounds had come our way. The odd one had been deliberately fired in our direction to try and provoke one of us into firing back. That would have given them just the excuse they wanted to wipe us out. The RPA didn't like the United Nations being there and made no bones about it. What we needed to do now was get ourselves and our gear quickly, quietly and safely packed on to our vehicles. Hopefully then we could leave this place in one piece.

As we gathered up what was left of our medical supplies and personal gear, we could see hundreds and hundreds of dead bodies littering the ground. We could hear the injured crying out in pain. But there was nothing more we could do that day to help these people. We had to get out while it was still daylight, or we might never get out at all. We could only hope the RPA would let us leave after what we had just witnessed. They had just murdered thousands of unarmed, starving, thirsty and helpless men, women, and children. Even babies had not been spared. Some of those who had survived the lethal onslaught of 50 caliber machineguns, AK47 rifles, rocket-propelled grenades and mortars were ruthlessly hunted down and bayoneted to death where they lay injured. We had just witnessed what became known as the "Kibeho Massacre". Would the Rwandan Patriotic Army allow witnesses to this atrocity leave the Kibeho refugee camp and tell the world what had happened? Or were they going to wipe us out as well?

I was one of 32 Australian soldiers in the area. We were facing more than 2,000 RPA soldiers. We were good, but not that good. The numbers were heavily in their favour. I was worried but I wasn't scared. All I had was questions. How the hell had a medical mercy mission ended in such a horrific tragedy? How had it been allowed to even get to this? Why were we not allowed to fire our weapons and defend these poor refugees? *God*, I thought, *I hope we live through this day. And if we do – I tell you what – won't I have a story to tell.*

11

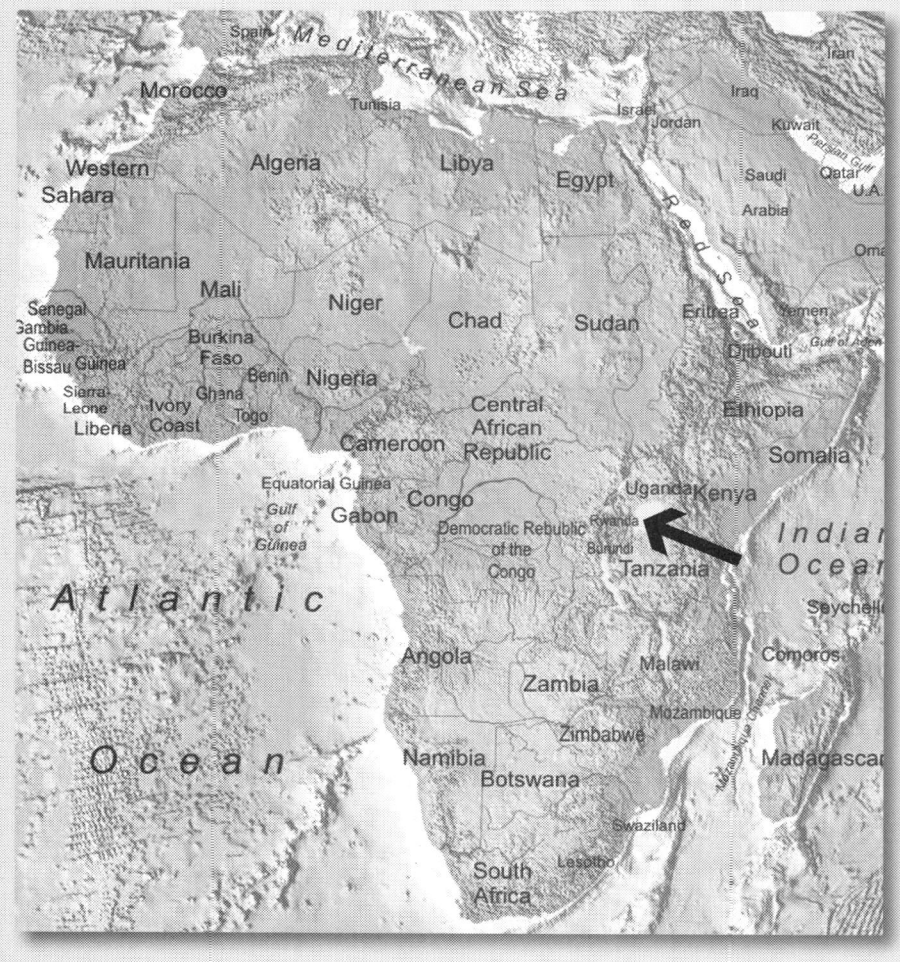

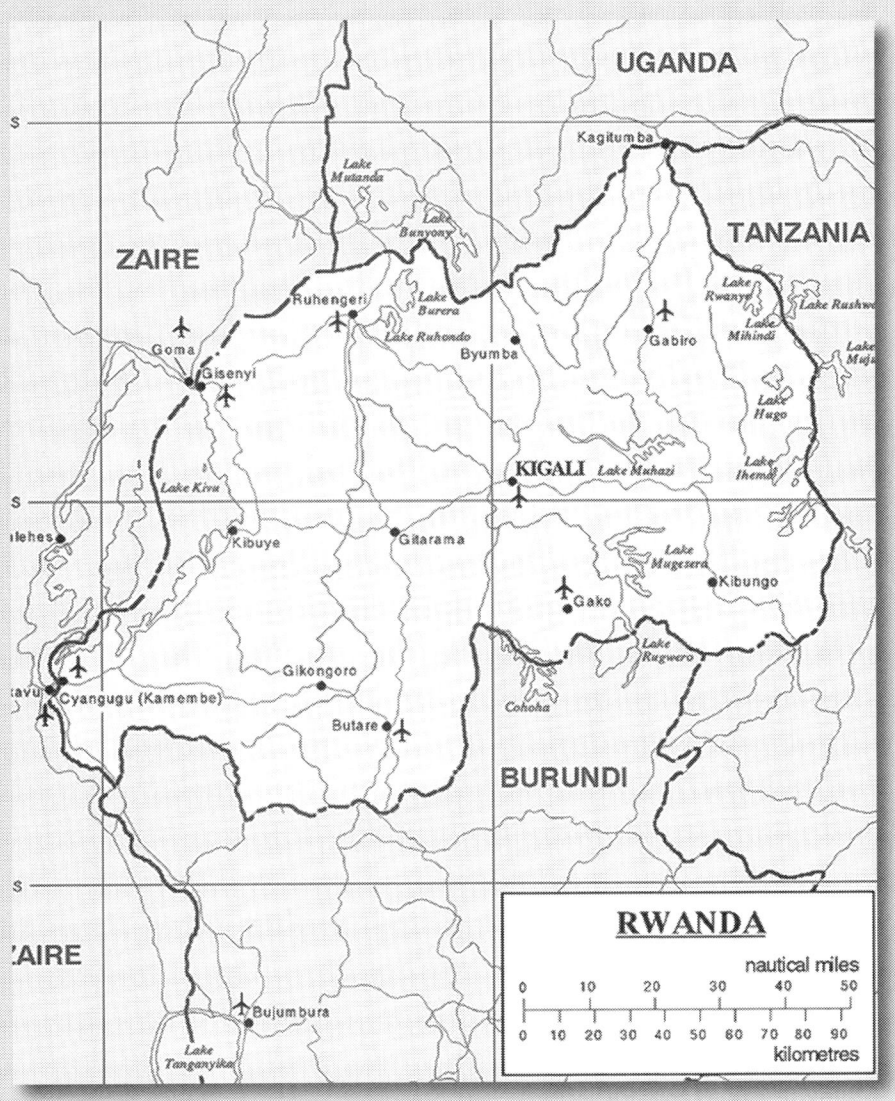

Chapter One

Soldier, medic

"When I returned to Tasmania I found myself at the army recruiting office in Hobart. I applied to join even though I had no idea what I wanted to do. I thought I could handle working as a soldier for 20 years if it meant that I could retire like my father had. And I would still be a young man at only 38. Stuff not wanting to kill anyone, I thought, and anyway the Vietnam War is over. Australian troops were not fighting anywhere at the time so I reckoned my chances of having to kill were slim."

I was destined to join the Army. For as long as I could remember my father was a soldier. He served in the British army before joining the Australian ranks. We moved around a lot. Whenever we arrived somewhere new I was faced with a familiar routine: new army house, new school full of army children, new army community. At one place even the public pool was run by the Army. Sometimes we crossed paths with people we knew who were moving around just like us. It wasn't as if I wanted to become a soldier. It was just meant to be.

At school I excelled at cadets. I loved the spit polish and the time we spent out bush. Drill was easy – anyone could follow orders. And I really enjoyed firing weapons when I had the chance. My older brother, Ken, joined the army reserve when he was old enough and then the regular Army as soon as he could. Most of the kids I grew up with joined the Army. The Vietnam War was on and all I ever saw on TV was the Army.

Yet I swore blind there was no way I was going to join the very organisation which had played such a big part in my life already. I believed that all life was precious. I didn't want to become a soldier and kill people. Some of the TV pictures coming out of Vietnam were very disturbing. A lot of people were dying horribly. I never understood why somebody would ever want to kill another person. Instead I wanted to do an apprenticeship in radio electronics. The problem was I had left school at the end of grade 10. To be accepted as an apprentice I would have to do another year. That was not going to happen. My dad wanted me to find a job so I could make my own way in the world. After working in a few different Hobart factories I ended up packing groceries and collecting trolleys at a Coles supermarket.

Not surprisingly, there didn't seem to be much of a future in any of the jobs I tried. They were all monotonous and boring. Sure, I made enough money to get by on my own but life was not leading me anywhere. My parents, Ken and Geraldine, had moved to South Australia and I was visiting one day when Dad told me he would soon be able to retire from the Army on a decent pension. To a 17-year-old that sounded pretty good considering he was only 45. He had served the 20 years in the Australian Army required to earn a pension and had reached the rank of captain in the Royal Australian Army Medical Corps where he was a quartermaster.

When I returned to Tasmania I found myself at the army recruiting office in Hobart. I applied to join even though I had no idea what I wanted to do. I thought I could handle working as a soldier for 20 years if it meant that I could retire like my father had. And I would still be a young man at only 38. Stuff not wanting to kill anyone, I thought, and anyway the Vietnam War is over. Australian troops were not fighting anywhere at the time so I reckoned my chances of having to kill were slim.

While the Army was a big influence in my life, it wasn't keen to have me full time. My application was rejected because they didn't think I was mature enough. The recruiters told me I should spend at least a year learning what life was about before trying again. After a couple more months working at Coles and a few more factories I had another go. This time they said they were not recruiting anyone from Tasmania! I kept working and saving and a month later flew to Melbourne to try my luck there. I was rejected again on the grounds that I was too young and immature. Next stop: South Australia and a glimmer of hope. "Reapply just before you turn 18," I was told, "and think about what you want to do." I thought I could be a medic. That way I wouldn't be trying to kill anyone, I would be fixing them instead. I applied again and was finally accepted, six months after my eighteenth birthday.

The twelve weeks of recruit training went by in the blink of an eye. It was a breeze. I easily handled the discipline and enjoyed the field work and weapons training as much as I had in cadets. I successfully applied for the Medical Corps and did my first course at the School of Army Health in the small, picturesque Victorian town of Healesville. I spent six months there doing what was a four-week course, and spent the rest of the time working in the gardens or as a steward in the officer's mess. The next seven months were spent at 2nd Military Hospital at Ingleburn near Sydney on a medical assistant course before my first posting to the 1st Australian Field Hospital nearby. In the first year I was promoted to lance corporal before accepting a posting on promotion to full corporal to the proof and experimental establishment at Port Wakefield in South Australia for two years. It was during this time that I met and married my first wife, Sue, and we had a son, Daniel.

After two years in my home state of South Australia we moved back to Healesville where I served as one of the only two corporal instructors at the School of Army Health. For the next two years I taught basic medical courses to new medical corps recruits, advanced first aid to the Special Air Service soldiers and basic first aid to other groups and courses around the state. Unfortunately, my family life wasn't going as well. Sue and I had married young and it wasn't working. We separated and Daniel and Sue moved closer to her Sydney family. It was the right thing for him because I was spending a lot of time away from home.

From Healesville I moved to Brisbane and the 1st Military Hospital at Yeronga where I became an instructor on the medical assistant training wing. By now I was one of the most senior corporals in the Medical Corps. But I had got into some trouble at Healesville and there was no chance of being promoted to sergeant until I proved I was a responsible corporal. I had shown poor judgment when I established a relationship with a student. It was wrong and I should have known better. My punishment was an administrative warning from the commanding officer. I had the option of proving my worth during the next six months or being discharged. My career was very important to me so I took it on the chin and set out to make amends. My chance came when I was selected for a three-month tour of duty to Malaysia with 8th/9th Battalion with two other medics. I also ran first aid instruction for several other units for which I was awarded a military skills award by the brigade commander.

Back in Australia I requested a posting to 8/9RAR as a company medic, even though I was told it would delay my chances of promotion for at least a whole year. I wanted the move because it meant I would be working more closely with infantry and would be the sole medic for an entire company – a real challenge. Twelve years had passed since I joined up and I was determined to earn that promotion. I learned fast and did a good job. It was good enough for them to put me on the courses I needed to do to become a sergeant. I passed easily and accepted a posting on promotion to sergeant to the School of Artillery at Manly in Sydney.

Two rather boring years spent mainly doing sick parades and paperwork was alleviated by the more enjoyable task of first aid instructing around Sydney, including the water transport unit. I missed the bush work that I'd enjoyed in my time with the infantry, but I was revelling in being a sergeant at long last. Life at home was also looking up. I had met Tara in Brisbane before moving to Sydney and we were married. Our wedding reception was held in the sergeant's mess.

After two years I accepted a posting back to Brisbane, this time to the 2nd/14th Light Horse Regiment in Enoggera. This was my type of unit. We were often out bush in APCs and I still taught first aid to other units as well as ours. I completed the APC driver and crew commander's courses which helped me teach military skills along with medical ones. I excelled in this environment and was soon nominated to do some of my warrant officer's courses. I passed easily.

It was about this time that I began to follow the United Nations missions. I had previously been accepted to go to Namibia as a medic while I was a corporal in 8/9RAR, but the mission ended before I left. My brother Ken had served as a medic in Cambodia and the UN mission in Somalia had just swung into action. I wrote to the head of the medical corps, volunteering myself for a UN mission. By now all I wanted to do after 15 years in the army was go on one of these missions and test my skills as a medic and a soldier in a hostile environment. It didn't look like there was much on the horizon so I thought the next best thing was the unit survival instructor's course in Darwin. It was one of the hardest courses around. Some failed the course, but I passed. I was ready for anything. While in Darwin I heard talk of a UN medical mission to a country in Africa I knew nothing about. Rwanda.

Chapter Two

Pre-deployment

"*A lot of questions were running through my head. Am I a good enough medic? Am I a good enough soldier? Am I fit enough? How well will I cope, working under pressure? What will it be like there? Is it possible that I might die? Who will look after my family while I am away?*"

I arrived at Brisbane airport from the Northern Territory late in the afternoon of September 22nd, 1994. The first thing I did when I got home was call my unit, 2nd/14th Light Horse Regiment, to confirm I had the rest of the week off. Waiting for me was a message to urgently call my squadron commander. He told me I had been nominated to go to Rwanda for the next rotation, but not to get my hopes up because it was only a unit nomination. Tara was really pissed off. I had just been away for a month and she was three months' pregnant. But, deep down, I was excited at the prospect of going on a UN mission. This was the sort of thing I had spent my career training for.

The list of personnel for the second Rwandan contingent was supposed to be announced on November 15th, but had to be delayed for more than a week while Parliament approved the rotation. On November 24th my squadron commander told me the list had been released and that nobody from Enoggera was on it. I was really disappointed, but at least I had an answer. That morning in the sergeant's mess one of my mates joked that the only place I would be going now was the School of Army Health to teach the new medics who would be going to Rwanda instead of me. The disappointment didn't last long. I was having physiotherapy for an elbow injury on December 9th when my commanding officer called. There had been a change to the deployment list. I was definitely going and could expect a posting order within the week. I went home to tell Tara but I think deep down she was already resigned to me going. Four days later my posting order arrived.

It was now time to get myself prepared. I had a dental check-up before facing my overseas medical board. As the unit's senior medic I had access to my own medical file. I was so determined to be on the UN mission I went through the file and removed anything I thought might be a concern for the doctor. Just in case! There was no need to worry. I was declared fully fit for overseas service.

My sergeant mates in the quartermaster's store equipped me with everything I needed before heading to Townsville for pre-deployment training: new uniforms, extra boots, even a second trunk. Passports were arranged and delivered. Blood was taken to make sure I didn't have HIV or Hepatitis B. A course of thirteen injections was supposed to help me fend off cholera, typhoid, tetanus and other nasties.

I also needed to be mentally prepared. A lot of questions were running through my head. Am I a good enough medic? Am I a good enough soldier? Am I fit enough? How well will I cope, working under pressure? What will it be like there? Is it possible that I might die? Who will look after my family while I am away? It was important to address each one of these questions and try to come up with a satisfactory answer, even if it was only for my peace of mind. The family situation was resolved by talking to army welfare, neighbours and unit staff. They would help look after my family by taking care of things like lawn-mowing and gardening. Neighbours would worry about changing light bulbs or fuses. Tara's mother would be there at the birth of our child which was due in late March. I also had to accept that all these questions and the self-doubt I felt were quite normal. As I worked through each question in my mind I made sure I got some sort of answer. Was I good enough? Well, I must be to have been nominated for overseas deployment in the first place, let alone be accepted. I was the sergeant in charge of the regimental aid post for my unit. I had been an instructor for years. I had already served 17 years in the Royal Australian Army Medical Corps and had nine postings ranging from hospitals to infantry battalions, artillery units to aviation and even water transport. Hell, I had even served with the Infantry Rifle Company in Malaysia for three months. If I didn't have enough medical knowledge and experience by now then something was seriously wrong. No one could argue I wasn't fit enough. I had never failed any of my physical training or swim tests. I always passed battle efficiency tests and had played a variety of sports in my time. I had run nearly every day of my army career, completed four marathons and done four ultra-marathons. At 35 I was one of the fittest soldiers in my unit.

What would it be like there? To answer that question I read everything about Rwanda I could get my hands on. My unit's intelligence section came up with different briefs as well. I attended every presentation about overseas service that Army Community Services gave and was ready to soak up everything I could learn during pre-deployment training in Townsville from soldiers who had already been to Rwanda. As for coping under pressure, I had received the best possible training that the Army and Medical Corps could give. I had never failed any of my promotional courses. I had just finished the unit survival instructor's course in the NT outback and been recommended to return in the future as an instructor. I had been the only medic on the scene treating injured soldiers more times than I could remember, so I was sure I could do my job. Now it was a case of wait and see. Was I a good enough soldier? I believed I was. It is possible to be an outstanding medic without being such a good soldier. There are medics who have never served in a field unit or outside of a hospital environment. I had served all over the place. I was a qualified driver and had passed driving courses for trucks, buses, cars and APCs (for which I was a qualified crew commander). I was one of only four members in my unit at that time qualified to instruct on the Steyr rifle and Minimi machinegun. I had already served as an infantry company medic doing everything they did as well as my own medical work. If all this experience didn't make me feel a little more confident then there was a problem.

Could I die in Rwanda? The answer, frankly, was yes. I coped with that by putting it into context with everything else in life. Hell, I could walk out the door and get run over, or suffer a heart attack tomorrow. This was my big chance to do the job I had been trained to do in a real war situation. That is what all soldiers really hope to do, so I was not going to let the little things bother me.

So I was in a good frame of mind after Christmas leave when I said goodbye to my family and friends and headed to Townsville. The majority of the second Rwandan contingent was from the north Queensland city. A company from the Townsville-based 2nd Battalion, the Royal Australian Regiment (2RAR) was providing major infantry security, so it made sense to have everyone go to 2RAR for the pre-deployment training. In the middle of January Townsville is really hot and humid and when I stepped off the plane I reminded myself to keep my fluids up. During the day the temperature regularly hits 35°C, and drops to around 25°C at night. It was perfect preparation for a mission to central Africa. I was allocated a room with a navy nursing officer theatre technician in a barrack block for sergeants and officers. He took the bed while I slept on a stretcher on the floor. I wasn't bothered. I had done this a thousand times before. And, quite simply, I was prepared to do anything to make sure I went to Rwanda. No one was certain of a place on the mission and there were extra soldiers training, including a sergeant medic, in case someone had to pull out due to illness or injury.

Pre-deployment training began at 0600hrs the next day. Physical training usually went for an hour followed by a shower, shave and breakfast at 0730hrs. Everybody ate in the same mess hall, and it wasn't unusual to find myself sitting with a digger from the infantry on my left and the company commander or another officer on my right. Briefings and lectures started at

0900hrs and because the medical company's lecture room was more than a kilometre away we started marching at 0830hrs to get there. This could be very uncomfortable in the unforgiving Townsville climate, particularly for those who weren't used to it. Early on a couple of the female air force nursing officers was taken ill and another fainted. It took about a week for us all to become fully acclimatised.

During the first couple of days we started to get to know each other. Medical company consisted of company headquarters, theatre, intensive care unit, ward, resuscitation bay, X-ray department, pathology, and Q-store. Each person in these sections knew what they had to do and that they had to do it well. Also within the medical company was an evacuation section made up of teams of two – a couple of air force medics and several Special Air Service Regiment (SAS) soldiers grouped into pairs. I bumped into the SAS soldiers and introduced myself. At the time my brother, Ken, was posted to the SAS Regiment in Perth. The medical company's sergeant major was also SAS and he ended up calling me Ken for most of the Rwandan tour. Then when we returned to Australia he started calling my brother Terry! I had worked with SAS soldiers in the past and had been an instructor on some of their patrol medic courses at Healesville. They were extremely efficient, very fit and probably the best soldiers in the Australian Army. I had a lot of respect for them.

The medical company had been drawn from 62 ADF units, a mixture of full-time and reserve army, navy and air force personnel. Among them were some old mates. Graham Boardman and I had served in 1st field hospital together in 1979. Graham was the spare sergeant training just in case one pulled out and unfortunately did not get to go. Lieutenant Robbie Lucas was an old student of mine from the course in Healesville in 1981. He had served as a medic before doing a nursing degree and then accepting a commission. Major Mary Brandy had been a captain in 1st Military Hospital in 1987 when I was a corporal medic. She would be my company's second-in-command and the senior nursing officer for the contingent. I knew a couple of other corporals from around the traps and several officers from other units. Lectures and presentations went all day with welcome breaks for morning and afternoon tea and an hour off for lunch. We marched back and forth to our lectures two or three times a day. We had lectures on medical procedures presented by army reserve specialists who had already been to Rwanda. Usually from big Australian civilian hospitals, these specialists' time was so valuable it was hard for them to get longer than six weeks away from work to help in a strife-torn country.

One of the most important things that needed brushing up was weapons training. Everyone in medical company had to be confident with their Steyr rifle because it would be their personal weapon in Rwanda. We would be carrying them in the loaded condition along with three magazines of live rounds for the entire tour. Graham and I were qualified Steyr instructors, so our medical company CSM told us to run weapons training after work each day to bring any personnel who weren't qualified up to speed. Some of the air force nursing officers had never even touched a weapon so we had to start the training from scratch.

It took us about a week of training for two hours every day after lectures before we were able to report to the CSM that we believed these people were experienced enough and, most importantly, safe enough to go on the range for a zero practice. When the range practice was conducted a couple of days later, with experienced sergeants acting as coaches for those firing weapons, it didn't go entirely to plan. After everyone in medical company zeroed their weapons it was my turn. Zeroing means customising the sights on your weapon so that the rounds hit the target you are aiming at. Each person is different and has to zero his own weapon. I fired my first group of five rounds into the target and when I moved forward to check it, I was amazed not to find any bullet holes. I checked the targets either side in case I had inadvertently aimed at them. Still nothing! Back on the firing mound I asked one of the RAEME soldiers to spot for me and fired my second group of five rounds. On moving forward once again I found no evidence of any rounds hitting the target. I was stunned. I was fully qualified on this particular weapon and had never missed a target in my life. Naturally it wasn't long before I started to get some smartarse comments about how good a coach I was when I couldn't even hit the target myself. When I fired the third group of five rounds my spotter saw a small burst of dust kick up on the extreme left-hand side of the range. He made some enormous adjustments to my sights before I finally had rounds hitting the target. It had taken me over 40 rounds to zero my own weapon! Afterwards all our weapons were packed into their crates ready to be put on the plane.

One of the most important presentations was by the legal officer on "Rules of Engagement" and "Orders for Opening Fire". He got a couple of the infantry sections to act as local Rwandan people and as an Australian rifle section. They gave us graphic demonstrations of when you were allowed to fire in self-defence and when you could not, and, importantly, how it related to our UN charter. If you fired a weapon without giving certain warnings, and could not clearly identify a direct threat to your life or the lives of those around you, it would be seen as murder by any military or civil court. This happened to British soldiers serving in Northern Ireland and they were found guilty of murder and sent to jail. Not surprisingly, all of us paid very close attention.

Even the Padre, who was going with us, had his turn. He held a service to bless the whole contingent and made himself available for anyone who might have religious or personal matters they wanted to discuss with him. He issued every member of the contingent with a small bible with a plastic cover that had the same camouflage pattern as our uniforms. After our company commander allocated each person to the section they would be working in, two afternoons were set aside so that we could all get to know each other a little better. The first thing I did was gather together the ranks that would be working in the ward. I got each person to talk a little about themselves. The first thing I noticed was that most of them were extremely disappointed to be working in the ward because it probably wouldn't be as exciting once we got to Rwanda. To be honest, so was I. They were a lot happier when I pointed out that at least we would have done our time in the ward when it came to the boss rotating us to new sections. Then it was time to meet all the officers who would be working in the ward. Each one was either a doctor or registered nurse. My job would be to look after the ward's administration and be the go-between for the officers and other ranks.

On one of our final mornings on Australian soil we received an up-to-date briefing on Rwanda from the intelligence section. It was, we were told, a landlocked country in East Central Africa approximately 20 degrees south of the equator. The country is equivalent to the area in Queensland that runs from the Gold Coast to the Sunshine Coast and across to Toowoomba. Its boundaries are shared with four other countries: Uganda, Tanzania, Burundi and Zaire. During the day the temperature tops 30°C, except in the highlands where it ranges from 12—15°C. We would arrive there just when the long rainy season from mid-March to mid-May was about to start.

We learned that for most of its history since the 15th century a Mwami or king had complete authority and the Watutsi, the forerunners of the current Tutsi tribe, had been the absolute rulers. In 1885 Rwanda became a German colony, but even then the Mwami continued to rule. After World War I the colony came under Belgian control until it gained independence in 1962.

During the 1950s the Hutu tribe began to resist the Tutsi monarchy and finally overthrew the king in 1959, forcing many Tutsis to flee to neighbouring countries. Gregoire Kayibanda became president and his party, the Hutu Emancipation Movement (PARMEHUTU), held power. In 1973 a bloodless coup brought in a new government led by Major General Juvenal Habyarimana, another Hutu, and a civilian-military government was installed. Habyarimana remained in power through four elections, the last being in 1988.

The Hutu-Tutsi conflict raised its ugly head again in 1990 when the Rwandan Patriotic Front (RPF), consisting mainly of Tutsis from Uganda, tried to topple the government. After three years of fighting, the two groups agreed to a ceasefire and a power-sharing agreement, but the fighting continued. In 1992 the Rwandan population was estimated at more than eight million and composed of 90 percent Hutu, nine percent Tutsi and one percent Twa (Pygmy). We learnt that the majority of people in the Rwandan capital, Kigali, were living in poverty and that hepatitis, dysentery, malaria and tuberculosis were rife. Just 50 percent of the people had access to safe drinking water. It was one of the poorest countries in the world. In 1993 the UN had again stepped in when the security council authorised a 2,550-strong United Nations Assistance Mission for Rwanda (UNAMIR) to supervise the peace accord. The assassination of Rwanda's president on April 6th, 1994, when his plane was shot down by rocket fire sparked a deadly wave of violence. The slaughter began in earnest. Ten Belgian peacekeepers were killed trying to protect the president. The Hutu military blamed the RPF, and used the president's death as the trigger for the revenge killings of the Tutsi. It is estimated in the three months after the assassination nearly a million Tutsis and moderate Hutus were massacred. The genocide only ended when the RPF and its Rwandan Patriotic Army (RPA) overthrew the Hutu government.

On 11th May, 1994, the UN Secretary General Boutros Boutros-Ghali said the UN was considering sending troops to Rwanda in the hope of ending the civil war. These troops would be permitted to defend themselves if attacked. Australia's contribution to this mission was medical support for the UN troops. We sent a fully equipped medical company, with an infantry rifle company for their security, and a support company. They served for six months. Although their primary role was to support the United Nations troops, there was a secondary role of providing humanitarian relief to the local people. My contingent was to replace them.

When the briefing was over the three companies went to designated areas to await the final address to be given by our commanding officer Lieutenant Colonel Damian Roach. He assured the medical company that this was our mission, and to have no doubt that the infantry and support companies were there to enable us to complete that mission in the safest and easiest way. He told us to do whatever it took to support the UN and that he would personally look after the rest for us. I felt so proud when he said this, considering he was an infantry officer who had just been posted from 8/9RAR to command us. By the end of the tour I got to know him fairly well. He also reminded us that the first contingent had a very hard time in Rwanda and would need time to come to terms with what they had been through. The country had seen too much death. It was hard for a nation to get itself together again when there were still corpses lying everywhere. The first contingent was forced to remove hundreds of bodies from the hospital just to be able to set up the medical facility. The infantry rifle company had to start the security process without any knowledge of what they were getting into. The first Australians had done a magnificent job, working to fulfil the mission statement under horrific circumstances. The colonel asked us to take all this into consideration when we arrived and not to say anything about what our soldiers might appear to be doing or how they had set things up. Basically, he wanted us to only say, "Well done" when we were doing our handover and not to give anyone a hard time. They were very much on the edge and the last thing they needed was someone from the new contingent mouthing off about anything.

Now there was little else to do but wait to be deployed. With all the training done, I felt ready and confident, although a little anxious. All I wanted now was to get over to Rwanda and do some "real" work. It felt good knowing that I had been chosen to go on this UN mission, and that it was a medical mission. Most of the previous UN missions Australia had been part of involved only a handful of medics amongst hundreds of armoured corps or signal corps soldiers. The mission in Cambodia, on which my brother had served as a medic, was basically a signals mission to set up communications. Somalia had been an armoured and infantry mission. Then the medics were supporting the other Australian troops. This time the medics were the ones being supported. The only thing left to do was pack our personal belongings and army kit into our trunks and hand them to the Q-store for transportation to the airport. Some air force personnel wanted to know if it would be all right to pack cans of shaving cream. Of course, I told them it was. Every soldier knows that if you pack shaving cream into trunks it's likely to leak on everything in the aircraft hold. I mischievously looked forward to them opening their foam-filled trunks in Rwanda.

We also spent half a day dipping our uniforms into large drums of Perigan which is supposed to remain in the material after it dries and act as a mosquito repellent. While we were doing this, each member of the contingent had their photo taken in front of the UN flag. When I asked the intelligence corporal taking the photos why we did this, he coolly told me it was so if anyone was killed they had an up-to-date photo to give to the media and, of course, the family. I thought, *That's a bit harsh, but fair enough.*

All that remained was to have our farewell parade where the Defence Minister and the Australian Army Land Commander would address us before we mounted buses for the journey to the airport. We were on parade and waiting for the dignitaries to arrive. After 40 minutes the Land Commander addressed us and revealed there was a problem with the plane. The radar system was not working and we would have to stay an extra night while the problem was fixed. Very early the next morning we finally arrived at the airport only to discover there was going to be a further delay of several hours apparently due to a hydraulic problem. There was nothing else to do but pick out a quiet area in the waiting lounge and sleep the time away. The plane belonged to Tower Air, which we nicknamed "Dodgy Brothers" because it seemed they were taking shortcuts to get the plane ready for takeoff. The Australian authorities were having none of this and we were not allowed to board until everything was in order. It was a frustrating period. All we wanted to do was get to Kigali where we would be based. While we waited, several soldiers told me they had read a short article about me in the *Sunday Mail* newspaper. Earlier that week some of us had been interviewed over the phone by the paper for stories they were writing about our deployment. I bought a copy and on page 22 was this article:

MISSION IN RWANDA FOR 300 AUSSIES

WHEN Tara Pickard gives birth in April, her husband Terry will be thousands of kilometres away in famine-struck Rwanda.

Sgt Pickard is in the contingent of 300 which left Australia last night on a six-month United Nations-chartered mission to provide medical aid to the people of Rwanda.

The Australian Medical Support Force – a mix of army, navy and air force personnel – flew out of Townsville last night on a 747 jumbo.

They will replace a contingent which has been in Rwanda for the past six months. The timing of the latest humanitarian mission means Sgt Pickard will not see his baby until he or she is four months old.

Tara flew up from Brisbane yesterday to be with her husband but their six-year-old daughter Alanna stayed at home. Having left Alanna three weeks ago when he flew up to Townsville for pre-deployment training, Sgt Pickard felt it would be too upsetting for her to say goodbye a second time.

He said he was disappointed not be able to be at the birth of his second child in April or to help his daughter celebrate her seventh birthday next month. But he was looking forward to working as a medical assistant at the Kigali hospital in Rwanda.

I ripped out the page and stashed it in my day pack so I could send it home later. After a boring seven-hour wait we were finally able to walk across the hot tarmac and climb the twenty-two steps to board the plane at 1250hrs. As we took off one of the central ceiling panels fell off and hit half a dozen soldiers on the head, luckily without injuring any of them. Half the plane's seats were shaky, several lights weren't working, and various bits of internal equipment were out of action. This, apparently, was how "Dodgy Brothers" operated. But even that didn't stop a big cheer going up from all the soldiers, sailors and airmen when we left the ground. We were on our way at last, and we had only lost about 27 hours! After a quick stop in Singapore, it was on to Nairobi before we finally landed in Kigali in the small hours of the morning. We were now safely deployed and in country.

Chapter Three

UNAMIR II

"The RPA soldiers stood around us, eyeing us up and down while they fidgeted with their AK47 rifles. One of them kept staring at the civilian Red Cross representative with us. He came up to me slowly and asked who she was. I told him she was with the Australian Red Cross and that she belonged with us. He looked her up and down a few more times before moving off slowly. We quietly shuffled her into the middle of our group. We hadn't forgotten that in the past ten months these people had killed ten UN peacekeepers and also attacked some UN Children's Fund (UNICEF) representatives."

After a long and tiring 18-hour flight we finally arrived at Kigali International Airport. We quietly disembarked and headed into the terminal. I could see the Australian infantry soldiers from the first contingent surrounding the building. They were fully kitted up with their weapons and wearing flak jackets and helmets. During my time in the Army I saw a lot of airports. This terminal was different. There were no regular passengers and there was no machine noise – only soldiers, our own and the RPA, eyeing each other off. It was a fairly modern building but the atmosphere was eerie. It was silent apart from the echo of 300 pairs of boots as we slowly made our way to customs. Everyone spoke in whispers. The damage the building had suffered during the war was clear to see. What little glass was left in the windows was full of bullet holes.

It was a slow two-hour process to get through Rwandan customs. Four Rwandan civilians working as customs officers were watched carefully by the RPA officer. And none of them were in any hurry. The RPA soldiers stood around us, eyeing us up and down while they fidgeted with their AK47 rifles. One of them kept staring at the civilian Red Cross representative with us. He came up to me slowly and asked who she was. I told him she was with the Australian Red Cross and that she belonged with us. He looked her up and down a few more times before moving off slowly. We quietly shuffled her into the middle of our group. We hadn't forgotten that less than a year earlier ten UN peacekeepers had been murdered, and there were attacks on some UN Children's Fund (UNICEF) representatives.

After what felt like an agonisingly long time, we were relieved to finally leave the building and board our trucks for the 40-minute drive to the Australian headquarters compound. Some of the soldiers, including me, started taking photos of the outside of the terminal. We were abruptly reminded by the CSM that the RPA didn't take kindly to any sort of photos being taken so we put our cameras away. It was probably a really good move since it was still dark and the flashes might have brought an unwelcome response. The drive through Kigali's dark, deserted streets was just as eerie as the airport. A few areas were lit by streetlights, but a lot were not. I didn't see a single person on the street.

Once inside the compound we dismounted and were immediately issued our weapons and ammunition. Some of the first contingent guided us to our lines where we could have a bit of a rest before starting the handover in the morning. We were already 27 hours behind schedule. It was 0300hrs and the handover of all positions was only four hours away because the entire first contingent was due to leave Kigali that afternoon. The commander of medical company, who had arrived two weeks earlier with the advance party, told me to go with him to the hospital compound at 0600hrs so we could start our ward handover before the rest of the staff arrived. There was no need for an alarm clock because very few of us slept and the Indian company which shared the compound started their early morning prayers at 0500hrs. The Hindu and Muslim prayers would go on loudly for about an hour before the Indians started work. Their primary role was providing engineer support to the whole UN mission. They also contributed to compound security by manning machinegun bunkers and assisting with front-gate security and night-roving picket.

The other ranks, corporal and below, shared a huge accommodation block with an Indian company. There were so many soldiers it meant living about ten to a room. The officers and sergeants had single rooms in a different block. I stored my gear in my room which consisted of a bed area against one wall, a locker, a sink and a shower cubicle. The previous occupant told me the water would be lucky to ever run, that the power cut out often and there was no way to secure the door. The glass in the door frame had been shot out the previous year. He gave me a good brief on how things worked and then headed off to get ready for his return to Australia. The room next door was allocated to Sergeant Eric Gutridge, a good friend of mine. Several years back we had served together in the military hospital and 8/9RAR. On this mission he was the preventative health team leader. He checked out his room and found several bullets under his sink left over from the war Rwanda had endured the previous year. All our rooms were pockmarked with bullet holes. I ended up using a panel marker to cover my door where the glass was missing. Eric used a piece of old cardboard.

I met Major Peter Wheatley, the medical company commander, at the front gate at the time arranged. To move from the headquarters compound to the hospital compound meant walking about 200 metres along the road outside. Everyone had to travel as a group or have at least two infantry soldiers for protection. Before leaving the compound our weapons would always be put in the loaded condition, which involved a safety check followed by placing a loaded magazine onto the weapon. It always pays to have a quick look at other soldiers' weapons to check that the safety locking device is in the correct position.

On arriving at any safe compound it was necessary to return your weapon to the unloaded and safe condition. This required you to remove the loaded magazine, cock the weapon, check that there were no rounds in the internal workings, release the working parts forward and then actually pull the trigger before placing the safety switch in the safe position. If this procedure wasn't carried out correctly there was a danger a round could be fired accidentally. Just inside the gates of each compound were small sandbag bunkers designed for this procedure which were nicknamed "Two Metre Ranges" due to the odd round being fired into them. This was classed as an unauthorised discharge (UD). Obviously, loading and unloading of weapons several times a day for six months can cause some soldiers to get a little lax. It was also costly. A UD would cost the perpetrator more than US$1,000 in fines.

Major Peter Wheatley and I walked to the hospital compound with our escort. Entering the ward was a stark reminder of the damage war can do. This building was also peppered with bullet holes and there was a distinct lack of colour. Everything seemed dark and grey. Staff from the first contingent did a ward round, introducing me and Major Peter Wheatley to all the patients. Apart from three injured UN soldiers, the ward was full of civilians, mostly injured children. A ten-year-old girl, nicknamed Missy, had lost a leg and eye after stepping on a landmine. Her mother died in the explosion, but Missy somehow survived. The three soldiers were from the Tunisian battalion and had been injured when a member of their section stood on a mine. That soldier had died and these three had each suffered more than a hundred fragmentation wounds to their legs. One of them also lost an eye. Another two had been evacuated to Nairobi with traumatic amputations. A walk through the rest of the ward revealed more horrific gunshot wounds or mine blast injuries. In that first 30 minutes I saw more patients with traumatic injuries than I had in my previous 17 years of Army service. It was a shock to the system and I was glad I had a chance to absorb it all before the rest of the ward staff arrived.

The handover went smoothly and I was appointed the new ward sergeant. As I walked around the small office I was amazed by how good a job the first contingent had done of converting this wing of Kigali Central Hospital into an Australian facility. When they first arrived the whole ward was full of rotting bodies that needed to be removed before it could be cleaned up and beds and other equipment brought in. I passed on as many "Well dones" as I could before bumping into a few of the medics I had come to know over the years. It was good to see them but they all looked tired. They were very happy to be finally going back to Australia.

The rest of the new staff started arriving and settling in. The first thing some of them did was meet in the brew room and make coffee before starting work. One of the air force nursing officers could find only UHT milk in the fridge. She asked one of the first contingent if there was any real milk because she really didn't like the taste of long-life milk. "Where the hell do you think you are?" he snapped. "We are in the middle of fucking Africa, so where the hell do you think they could get real milk from?" The nurse quietly slipped away and was never heard complaining about milk again.

I spent the rest of the day working out the shift roster with the head nursing officer, an air force captain. We started with 12-hour shifts just to get things settled. I made sure the medical stocks were up to date and made a start on reducing the paperwork by throwing away anything that appeared to be duplicated. When the rest of the staff arrived I gave them their tasks and made sure all the patients were okay. Missy needed her dressings changed and I told one of the young air force nurses to do it. She went away and got everything, but returned a few minutes later to tell me that she wasn't sure if she could do it. She had never seen such wounds and just looking at them made her feel ill, so I downed tools and went to help. Missy had at least 50 shrapnel wounds and it took us quite a while to change the dressings. After that I always allocated two medics or nurses to do dressings until everyone was used to the sight of the wounds.

Meals were brought over in hot boxes from the headquarters compound by kitchen staff and handed out to the patients, and any leftovers were given to the on-duty staff. The CSM had this changed in the first week so that patients and staff had their own boxes. Specialists, the company commander, the CSM, and on-call evacuation and resuscitation teams had to be at the hospital all the time. They stayed in rooms on the first floor above the ward. The infantry soldiers from the platoon who remained at the hospital compound supplied stretcher teams and pack storemen for the resuscitation room and had a separate area of their own.

Four locals, two men and two women, worked for us as interpreters. The men were at the hospital 24 hours a day. The women came in early in the morning and left each afternoon. They all spoke very good English, French, Rwandese and Swahili. Whenever a patient needed anything one of the interpreters helped us communicate. It took a while to get used to this system but it was a good way to start learning some of the language.

All medics took turns on the two on-call resuscitation teams which consisted of a doctor, nursing officer and two medics. Team Alpha stayed at the hospital and Team Bravo stayed at the headquarters compound ready to go to the hospital if required. 'Resus A duty' basically meant sleeping at the hospital to await the arrival of any casualties. The on-call team had a room to sleep in and I found it extremely stressful just lying down and waiting, listening to footsteps coming towards the room and wondering if they were coming to get us. The echoing footsteps got louder as they approached the room, and the closer they got the faster my heart would beat in anticipation of being called out for a resus. Sometimes the footsteps carried on past the door and my heart rate would slow down again as I tried to settle back to sleep. Other times the footsteps stopped before there was a knock on the door. After literally bouncing out of bed, I would dress as fast as I could (sometimes not even doing up my bootlaces) just to get down to the resus bay, hopefully before the injured person arrived. Most of the people requiring resuscitation had been horrifically injured by mines, car accidents, gunshot wounds and the occasional grenade. A lot were saved only because of the excellent resus ability of the standby resuscitation teams. Once the casualty left the resus bay they would go to theatre or the intensive care unit. Then it was up to us to clean up the blood and old clothing, change linen and restock the emergency supplies. Once in a while a severed limb had to be removed, or perhaps the body of someone who didn't survive. After a debrief it was back to the room, hopefully to get a little undisturbed sleep. During one 24-hour period that I was on duty, we had seven resuscitation casualties. During my six-month tour I did 29 Resus Team A and 13 Resus Team B duties. The evacuation teams consisted of a driver and medic, usually from special forces. Their job was to collect casualties from a variety of places, including the airport, and stabilise the casualty en route to the hospital where they would then be sent to the resus bay. There was always a team at the hospital on standby and three other teams at the headquarters compound – all special forces soldiers who were medically qualified and ready to move at a moment's notice.

The first few days in Rwanda were spent working flat out. I worked for 41 hours in the first three days and 83 hours by the end of the first week, including my first day off. One day sticks in my memory. We had five resuscitations, a sharp increase in the number of patients admitted to the ward, and a young girl died of complications arising from tuberculosis causing respiratory failure and cardiac arrest despite the best efforts of two special forces medics performing CPR. The CSM, Scotty, had to get her body ready for viewing and removal by her family. To make room for her in the morgue fridge I had to remove several bags of body parts and take them to the incinerator for burning. Just before the family arrived, Scotty and I quietly and respectfully washed her, and then stood by with bowed heads and solemn thoughts as her family tearfully paid their last respects and then took her away for burial. She was just nine years old.

Taking body parts to the incinerator, which was located in the Rwandan part of the hospital, required a fully armed infantry escort. Sometimes the soldiers would ask what I had in the bags. When I told one young soldier he said there was no way he would help me carry them. After struggling 300 metres with my arms full, I decided it was easier to tell them it was rubbish. That way I at least got some help.

At the end of each day everybody back in the headquarters compound had to line up for their evening meal. It took about 40 minutes to get to the serving point before heading for the large dining room. One evening, while I was waiting in line, I heard the shower generator start up. The generator converted cold water into hot and pumped it through pipes into a makeshift shower room. We could shower on Saturday, Monday and Wednesday; the men 5—5.30pm and the women 6—6-30pm. The generator was so loud you had to shout to be heard. On this day I sprinted off to have my shower and still managed to make it back in time for dinner because the queue was so long.

My next door neighbour, Eric, was a very thrifty person. He had brought a sewing machine from Australia on the off-chance that some of the soldiers might need patches sewn onto their uniforms. We had all been issued UN patches and the medics had also been issued red crosses. Eric got busy with his machine and was soon backed up with orders. Sometimes he would work until midnight. Of course, there was a small payment to Eric for the service.

Some of the drivers, myself included, were irritated by the time spent getting in and out of vehicles. We constantly had to put our webbing on and take it off, and when you don't have your webbing, you have no spare ammunition magazines handy. Some of us carried small radios for communication when we were outside the compound. With this also in the webbing, it made it hard to hear what was going on. Naturally, Eric had the solution. With permission from the commanding officer and the RSM, he started making chest webbing. He drew a pattern on cardboard and started mass producing green and UN blue chest webbing. He churned out three sets in one night and it wasn't long before chest webbing became commonplace. Just another donation to Eric's family fund.

Working in the ward got easier as time passed and people got used to the routine, so shifts were reduced to eight hours. I still liked to get to the hospital early to make sure there were no problems with the night staff and to attend the morning handover. Patients came and went, most of them children injured in mine explosions. We cared for UN soldiers and even the odd RPA soldier. The three Tunisians were there for quite a while before being discharged and returned to their unit for repatriation back home. I have always been pretty good at communicating with people from other countries by using a combination of hand gestures and sign language but for some reason I just couldn't work out what one of the three Tunisians was after. I asked if it was water or food, or something to read, but he just kept shaking his head. No matter what I tried I could not get his meaning. The interpreters couldn't help either. The Tunisian people are not shy about holding hands as a sign of friendship, much like young girls in Australia might. I found myself being walked down the ward with one of them holding my hand. I copped quite a few wolf whistles from my staff as I entered the tea room holding hands with this soldier. He took me to the fridge and showed me that he wanted milk. For the next week or two my fellow sergeants stirred me up, sending me flowers and saying that they were from the Tunisian soldier. One even wrote a fake invitation inviting me to live in Tunisia. It took a while to live it down.

Two weeks before Easter the RSM, Alan Castle, after hearing of Eric's sewing prowess, asked if he would be able to make a bunny suit. The RSM wanted to do something nice for the CARE Australia orphanage. Eric took up the challenge and started work that very night. He figured the hardest thing to make would be the rabbit's head and so spent most of his time on that. After finishing the head, he made mittens for hands and used white plastic protective overalls as the body. The feet were the only thing he couldn't work out. You couldn't have a pair of army boots so I suggested the protective overboots worn by theatre when they operated on patients. A couple of days later the RSM said he would volunteer a digger to wear the suit but after some discussion I decided I'd do it. Naturally, within a few minutes Eric managed to give the good news to half the sergeants and the public relations officer, Major Seaman, who decided that he would make a little film out of the whole show to send back to Australia. He thought that some footage of Eric making the suit and then me wearing it around the barrack block would be a good place to start. After about 10 minutes I became aware of several issues. Firstly, I could see bugger all and would need an escort to guide me around. And secondly, it was extremely hot.

Major Seaman also thought it would be a great idea if we went to the local Mother Teresa's orphanage a week before Easter so he could get the footage of our humanitarian work back to Australia in time. Fine by me, I thought, it'll get me out of working in the ward for a day. So off we went with the suit in an echelon bag. After about an hour of playing with the children, I slipped away to an unused room to change. Five minutes later I emerged to the delight of the sisters and the other hospital staff who had come with us. Unfortunately, some of the children didn't know what to make of this giant, white bunny since they had never seen one before. The two-year-olds ran away screaming and hid amongst the sisters' legs, but as soon as I started to hand out chocolate they cautiously returned. Some of the older kids came up to me and stared into my eyes and asked if I was a "muzungu" or white man, but I surprised them by speaking in their own language. After about two hours of being led around by the hand by one of the nurses because I couldn't see anything, I returned to the room to change and nearly passed out from dehydration. I had been sweating profusely for two hours inside the plastic suit without a drink. Two litres of water went down in a flash. The day turned out to be a huge success and the grateful sisters thanked us as we helped clean up all the lolly and chocolate wrappers before returning to the hospital.

The following week I headed to the local disused golf course for an Easter barbecue with children from the orphanage run by CARE Australia. There was no shortage of soldiers volunteering for this job, with at least an infantry platoon and all the off-duty nurses helping out. The Canadian contingent supplied the trucks to pick up more than a hundred children and as they began to arrive we could hear them all chanting "Australia, Australia". As I listened I thought to myself, *This is going to be a really good day*. A few of us got the barbecue going and soon had sausages sizzling while others buttered bread rolls. We handed out soft drinks to the children and played soccer and football with them as well as chasing and running games. The kids were having a ball but the real surprise was still to come. I slipped away with one of the nurses to change into the bunny suit. It came as a complete surprise when I came out and waved to all the children. The commanding officer of our unit and the RSM hadn't seen the suit and were impressed as was everyone else. My guide led me around as I handed out Easter eggs to all the children and staff, including our commanding officer. He quietly gave it back, telling me to give it to one of the kids. It was another hot day and I was wilting inside the suit but Major Seaman, always keen for a story, wanted a photo session with the kids, some of our soldiers and CARE Australia staff. I made a deal with him and the photos were taken with the rabbit head off! It was another hour before I could ditch it. This time I drank three litres of water and felt a little ill for the rest of the day, but it was worth it. A couple of weeks of fun had broken up the monotony of working in the wards.

The UN was heavily involved in Rwanda at the time and it was necessary for some of us to visit other UNAMIR units around the country. These trips were more for goodwill than anything else but we jumped at any chance for a change of scenery. They also gave us the advantage of being able to gather local intelligence for our intelligence section. Information from different areas gave the section some insight into how the whole country was going, and hopefully whether there was any imminent threat to us or other units. My CSM tasked me to gather any information I could and write a report when I returned. My first trip was to Ruhengeri and Gisenyi up north to visit the Tunisian battalion, and this was the report:

"On 8 March 1995 I was the medic allocated to a small contingent of Australian Medical Support Force (AMSF) to do a two-day reconnaissance of Ruhengeri and Gisenyi. We travelled in a convoy of four vehicles, one 6 by 6 Land Rover, one FFR, and two Land Rovers GS with a trailer. The team consisted of twelve infantry for protection, eleven operational support personnel including three operational headquarters staff and myself as the medic. The route taken was the 'Blue Route' to Ruhengeri and then on to the 'Maroon Route' to Gisenyi, firstly heading north-west then south-west.

"'MSR Blue' is a very hilly distance of one hundred kilometres from Kigali to Ruhengeri with some gradients of 7.5% and 8%. The road is a double lane highway with white centre lines and is a sealed bitumen road. There are numerous potholes and several small rock slides along this route but these only cause minor delays. Only one roadblock was encountered twenty-five kilometres from Kigali with the RPA not holding up any United Nations vehicles.

"'MSR Maroon' is also hilly and is a distance of sixty kilometres from Ruhengeri to Gisenyi. This road is also sealed and in a reasonably good state

of repair although once again there are numerous potholes and rock slides. There are roadblocks both in and out of Ruhengeri and another one about ten kilometres before Gisenyi. There was no delay at Ruhengeri and a five minute delay at the last roadblock as the RPA moved other trucks out of the way to allow us through. Both 'MSR Blue' and 'MSR Maroon' experience delays due to the movement of herds of cattle down the roads. The RPA appear much more disciplined and friendly in this area.

"Medical Facilities

"On 'MSR Blue', approximately thirty-five kilometres from Kigali in a small town named Tare, was a dispensary sign and a Red Cross sign with an arrow pointing to a building on the left hand side of the road. As far as I could tell the building was completely deserted and derelict. Further on in a town named Nemba, approximately fifty kilometres from Kigali, I saw two local stretcher teams, one heading north into Nemba and the other heading south into Nemba which would indicate the presence of a reasonable medical facility. Unfortunately there were no signs to indicate this. There was also a Tunisian rifle company located in this area which is believed to have a medical section with them. At Ruhengeri there was a large local hospital with a dispensary on the left side of the MSR just on the entrance of town heading north. There also appeared to be a large UNICEF presence within the confines of this facility and there were at least twenty-five local people lined up at that dispensary. There was also a small hospital set up on the right hand side of the MSR heading north about five kilometres into Ruhengeri with some sort of United Nations presence. Both hospitals were clearly marked with red crosses and signs marked 'Hospital'. At Gisenyi we came across a very large presence of CARE that had a number of trucks. They were all parked waiting for something; I would say permission to cross the border. With them were also several trucks marked 'United Nations' and 'OIM' which were used to transport local refugees from one place to another, hopefully home.

"Tunisian battalion area

"We spent the night at the Tunisian battalion strong point area. This place was extremely well defended with weapon pits around the entire perimeter as well as deep trenches. All the weapon pits had overhead protection (OHP) and there was an observation point (OP) on the nearby hill, which was manned at all times with a full section of their soldiers. Around the clock there was at least a full section of soldiers in bulletproof vests and helmets fully armed with machineguns guarding the perimeter. Sandbag walls protected all shipping containers and important equipment such as generators, and the sandbagging was continuing even while we were there. The entire compound was surrounded with figure-eight barbed wire topped with three strands of razor wire.

"Tunisian medical facilities

"The strength of the Tunisian battalion was about nine hundred soldiers with five or six companies all located in various locations throughout their designated sector. Each company had a medical section, although I could not work out if each had a doctor attached. They had a resuscitation team set up at Ruhengeri, which was approximately twenty-five kilometres by road to the northwest. Their evacuation system was by road from initial contact through a regimental aid post (RAP) set up, then on to Ruhengeri, and, if needed, evacuated by helicopter through to the Australian hospital at Kigali. The Tunisians had an X-ray technician who would take patients to Gisenyi and use their X-ray machines there. They also had a pathology laboratory technician and a preventative health team, all of which belonged to the medical section under the command of a medical officer. In the one RAP I visited, the medical officer would see on average six United Nations soldiers a day. The medical section had set up another smaller RAP outside the perimeter wire for checking the local Rwandan people who needed treatment and on average would see one hundred and fifty to two hundred people a day. The Tunisians were trying to teach the locals basic hygiene and were endeavoring to put up posters for this purpose. While I was there I met two captain medical officers, one medical staff sergeant, one sergeant, and several medical corporals. It appeared that each of their companies had the same medical facilities although I still could not find out if each had a doctor. The health and hygiene of the entire area was of a very high standard with toilet and shower facilities that were being cleaned on a daily basis. There was ample water supply including potable and non-potable water that was tested each day.

"Tunisian Soldiers

"The morale of all the soldiers was really good and their hospitality excellent. While we were there we were challenged to a game of volleyball and a game of soccer, both of which the Tunisians won. The commanding officer invited us all for dinner in the officer's mess which ended up being a four-course *meal of local Tunisian food. They even supplied breakfast the next morning, which was better than the French ration packs we had been issued. As it was raining heavily the commanding officer allowed us to stay and sleep on the floor in the officer's mess.*

"The trip to Gisenyi was very educational both medically and militarily. The local people along the roads we travelled along at times appeared quite well off with nice clothing, food and housing, but then within one kilometre there were other children begging with clothes literally falling off them. There was a lot of housing that appeared unused and empty, awaiting the return of refugees, most of whom would not be returning because they had been killed during the previous year's massacre. There were designated water points along the road with lines of people waiting to fill up their yellow jerry cans, most of them children. In one river I saw people washing clothing and bathing and further downstream people collecting water in their yellow jerry cans. In all of the mountainous areas some of the tops of the mountains disappeared into the clouds. Even so they were all still farmed all the way up to the top. Most people, especially the children, were always friendly, waving and smiling as we drove past. Most were heading to markets to either buy or sell farm produce. The RPA in this area were always friendly towards us and did not hinder us in any way apart from the odd roadblock. The RPA presence was very high throughout all areas with carloads and truckloads travelling in both directions up and down the road."

When I returned to the hospital I typed my report into the computer and handed it in to the CSM, who no doubt would have read it and then handed it on to the intelligence section. That was the last I saw of it. I went back to working in the ward until the sections were changed around and I was allocated to the casualty clearing post (CCP) which was nowhere near as hectic as the wards. As the sergeant my task was to ensure all the equipment was in working order and the supplies were always up to date so that the CCP could be deployed at a moment's notice.

I was joined at the CCP by Corporal Milan Nikolic and Private Franks, Lieutenant Robbie Lucas as the nursing officer, and Captain Carol Vaughan-Evans as the doctor. Our work in Rwanda was to give as much medical care to the local people as we could, as long as it did not interfere with our mission. The CCP would go to the local orphanage and run sick parades for the children. We began an inoculation programme which we hoped to finish by the time we left the country. The orphanage was run by the sisters of

Mother Teresa, who were always happy to see us and keen to talk for hours. If there was not a lot to be done in the CCP I would ask the corporals to work a half-day in the ward, and I sometimes worked there myself. The ward was always busy and extra help was always welcome. However, it wasn't long before another trip needed a medic, and once again my CSM asked for a full report.

"On 29 Mar 95 I was designated medic for part of a group of Australian soldiers that was to visit a church at Ntarama which is approximately thirty to forty kilometres south of Kigali, the capital of Rwanda. We travelled in a convoy of four vehicles making sure that we carried our weapons at all times. The driving time was about one hour and fifteen minutes on reasonable dirt roads. Prior to leaving the bitumen road one of our 6 by 6 vehicles broke down with some sort of fuse problem consequently there was a forty-minute delay while it had it be driven back to Kigali for repairs and eventually to be replaced with another vehicle. During our wait I saw a local person remove the numberplates from a shot up VW Kombi that had been dumped on the side of the road and place them on his own Mazda 626. Two UNHCR buses were seen travelling towards Kigali, one was empty and the other was full of local people travelling with all their personal belongings. At 0948hrs I saw a very well kept, light green truck which appeared to be carrying an artillery piece heading south, probably going to Kibeho. There were six RPA soldiers all armed with AK47s and a driver with a passenger. It could be assumed that this artillery piece was from Kigali as we had seen it there before, however it was covered with a tarp although the barrels were visible. Upon checking later I found out it was a ZPU-4 anti-aircraft machinegun. After our replacement vehicle returned we left the sealed road and travelled one or two kilometres along a well-worn dirt road to be confronted with the first RPA roadblock. Beside the roadblock was an 11 by 11 tent, which housed RPA soldiers. The roadblock was made of a pole placed across the road and fifty metres past this roadblock was lengths of razor wire to stop people, in particular refugees, getting through. After being checked we then proceeded a further fifteen kilometres to a river crossing. The bridge was made of prefabricated steel so it was quite safe to cross and would have been twenty-five metres in length. The river had a very strong current. On the southern side of the bridge was another roadblock, this one being made simply of string. We were only quickly checked and were able to proceed on our way. A few kilometres further we came across a very strong presence of RPA and they all appeared very friendly. We drove past Infirmary Du Ninda, which is classed as a local

hospital with dirt floors, and in very poor condition. I would hate to have to go there myself for treatment or even send any of my soldiers there since it was in such poor condition. After another two kilometres we finally reached our destination at Ntarama. We tried to gain entry into the compound that housed the church but were refused entry by a local RPA guard. Both gates had been recently padlocked and a new fence erected. A vehicle with a South African journalist pulled up beside us to tell us we would not be able to gain access to the compound because we would have to get written permission from a local prefector or councillor. Obviously that was not possible so we could only look through the fence. In front of us we could see an area of approximately eighty metre frontage and two hundred metre depth with a two metre high fence newly erected to stop people entering without permission. The fence was obviously new and had two sets of double gates that were double padlocked. As we were denied access we decided to take photos but with local RPA soldiers turning up all photography was banned. I borrowed a pair of binoculars to gain a better look at the church building that had now been set up as a memorial for the people that had been massacred inside it during the 1995 massacre. It was now considered a shrine of remembrance for the poor unfortunate people who had been killed. With the binoculars I could clearly see into the compound and saw a large table outside the church building. The church had a large iron cross on its roof peak. On the table I could clearly make out ten to twenty rows of skulls of the victims of the massacre. A lot of the skulls had been obviously shot; some had been macheted while they were still alive. Under the table were many different types of bones some still with bits and pieces of clothing on them. There was also a very large pile of bodies covered with white cloth. The table was covered by a temporary lean-to for protection from the weather and this was in a bad state of repair. As we all stood at the front gate we could identify several pieces of vertebrae scattered on the ground around us directly under our feet. It very soon became apparent that the binoculars were causing some concern with the RPA soldiers who actually thought that it was a camera so I quickly hid them in amongst my rations. They were not able to find them and soon after left us alone. Inside the compound there were four buildings, two of which had obvious structural damage from artillery and mortar fire. There were two buildings behind the church, one of which was made or repaired with large mud bricks as opposed to the normal bricks. All the buildings had corrugated iron roofs that did not appear damaged in any way so had probably been just renovated. Further behind the two smaller buildings was a wooden-poled lean-to with a corrugated iron roof. In the front area of the compound was a round water tank made of rock and cement which was about two metres diameter and two metres tall. It had two pipes, one of which I assumed to be the inlet and the other the outlet for water. I was reasonably sure that there was some sort of water supply to the area as I had seen two similar tanks just down the road. Along the fence line new work was being done with some areas of built up rock walls waiting to be cemented. Apparently this whole area was going to become a memorial to all the people who had been massacred in the church while they were celebrating mass. After thirty minutes we headed back to Kigali with the only difference on the way back being that first two vehicles were let through the roadblock and the second two, including mine, were searched. We hid all our cameras and got through the checkpoint after a quick search. We were pretty nervous because cameras could have been confiscated. Throughout the trip it was plain to see that this area of Rwanda was much poorer than the northern part of the country. People were dressed in much older clothing, some of them in rags. Overall there appeared to be a lot less farming and a lot less people around. Some areas had a bit of haphazard farming but most areas were not farmed at all. Most of the communes had few people in them and the majority of houses were either empty or completely run down. On the trip back to Kigali it rained and only twice did I see houses that had water tanks for collecting rain, very unusual for a country that appears always short of water. The local people we saw on the return trip were all waving and smiling at us as we drove past because they think we are their saviours and naturally we always waved and smiled back at them because they have had such a hard life in the last couple of years and probably will for the next couple as well."

I was finally issued with a UN driver's licence which allowed me to drive to and from the orphanage when I needed to run sick parades or deliver stores instead of tying up one of the transport drivers. One evening I was at the hospital when I received a phone call from the operations officer at headquarters asking if I had a UN licence. When I replied that I did, she said I would probably need it where I was going. I had no idea what she was talking about. The fact she had asked me the question made me feel that something was up.

I didn't know it at the time, but I was just about to spend a week in hell.

PERSONAL PARTICULARS

Page 1

Surname: PICKARD
Other Names: TERRENCE ROBERT *(In full)*
Army Number: 147815
Corps: RAAMC
Identity Card Number:
Date of Birth: 18 JUN 59
Place of Birth: SYDNEY NSW *(Town/State)*
Religion: CE
If Will lodged and where:
Complexion: FAIR
Marks or Scars: Hernia scar
Hair: L BROWN
Eyes: BLUE
Height: 178cm
Weight: 54 kg (lbs)

Physical Disabilities and Special Characteristics (eg. impediment of speech, allergies)

Date of Photograph: 22 Apr 1978
Marital Status:
Blood Group: O Pos
Signature: Terry Pickard

Above. Page one of my regimental records shows me on the fourth day at recruit training weighing in at a healthy 54kg. The section corporals had betsas to whether I would be strong enough to actually cock the self-loading rifle. I did, so they lost.

Below left. As an instructor at School of Army Health in 1980 I am setting up a parachute harness to simulate a suicide casualty. *Below right.* The casualty is used to represent a casualty and is hung in the toilet block for our students to find and react to try and save his life.

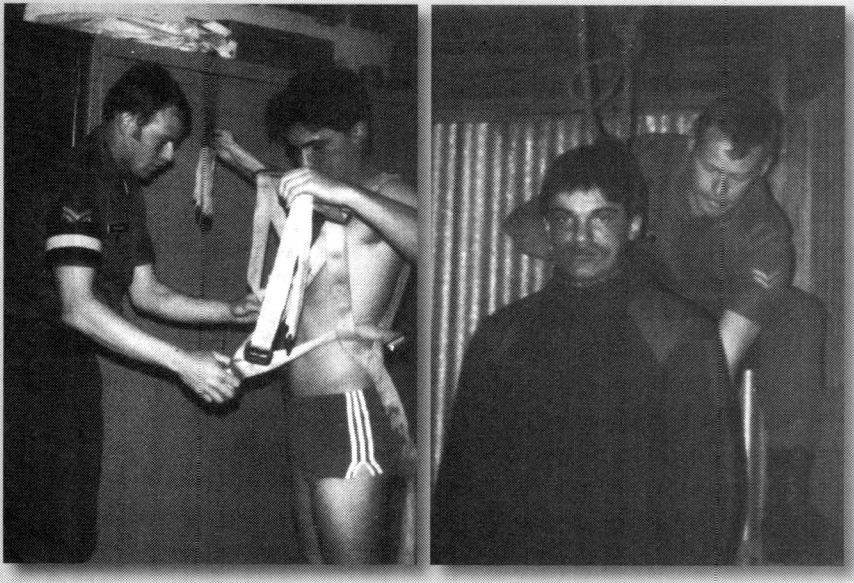

Above. Me (second from left) during the sea phase of the survival course. Hanging in the tree are bottles of water we procured by desalinating the sea water. We caught fish and ate some of the local plants. The fire was lit by rubbing two sticks together until a cinder was hot enough to start a fire. I burnt my hand severely when checking the hot water but didn't tell anyone.

Below. One of the doctors and me posing for the local newspaper at the RAP School of Artillery in 1990.

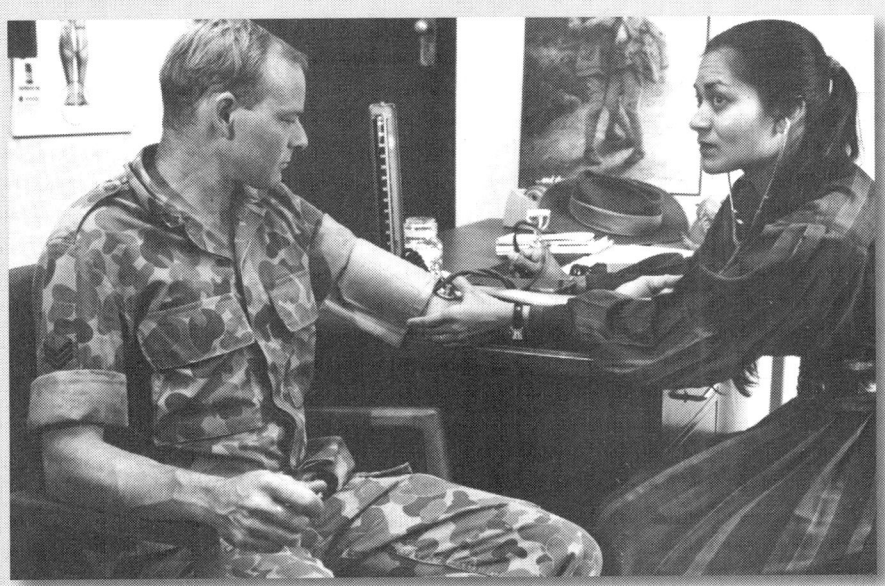

Above. Local ambulance used for range practices.

Above. The facilities at Landing Point 113.

Above. Heat exhaustion patient treated by Brunei medic and myself.

Above. Field Casualties had to be carried out by streacher to a landing zone.

Above. Unloading stores in Brunei. Because of the thick jungle and hilly terrain all work had to be done with the helicopters, including casevac.

Above. A chance to rest and dry out some clothing in Brunei.

Above. Writing orders in the rain for the jungle attacks in Brunei.

Chapter Four

Kibeho, hell on earth

"*It was horrific. The room was full of people with all sorts of terrible injuries. Some refugees were dead, others had shocking wounds caused by machete attacks and bullets. There were men, women and children ranging in age from just a few days to over 60. The floor was covered in blood and human waste. The stench was unbelievable.*"

On 18th April, 1995 at about 1600hrs the operations captain rang me from headquarters to ask if I had my UN driver's licence. She hinted that there could be a trip for the casualty clearing post (CCP) somewhere down south. I thought this was a bit odd and waited in the hospital compound for more information. It wasn't long before Captain Carol Vaughan-Evans, who was in charge of the CCP, rang me to say we were going to deploy to a refugee camp called Kibeho, about 150 kilometres south west of Kigali. The camp reportedly held around 150,000, mainly Hutu, internally displaced people (IDPs), who had been there since the 1994 genocide. The IDPs had sought sanctuary at Kibeho because they believed a miracle had occurred in the local church where three children claimed to have seen a vision of the Virgin Mary. The camp was well set up with small markets, food and water supplies provided by humanitarian relief groups as well as thousands of shelters.

I organised the loading of all CCP stores, including trunks of medical supplies, fuel, water, a large Trelleborg inflatable medical tent and rations. I re-called the other members of the CCP staff to the hospital to help out. Private Franks was on leave in Nairobi at the time so he was replaced by Corporal Tim Whyte from the regimental aid post (RAP). A registered nurse, Tim had chosen to be a corporal medic in the army reserve rather than take a lieutenant's commission and serve as a nursing officer. We all worked through the evening, checking and loading stores onto Unimog trucks and Land Rovers. Many off-duty staff helped and the medical CSM, Scotty, coordinated the job. Everyone was keen to help in any way they could, from Major Brandy to the soldiers working in the orderly room. There was an air of anticipation and excitement because we all knew it might be a dangerous mission that would test our soldiering and medical skills. It was always good to have a little danger in your life!

It was nearly midnight when we finished loading. Each of us then went to our own lines to organise personal equipment like rations, water and ammunition. All weapons were cleaned and inspected. Ammunition magazines were also checked to make sure they functioned properly. Once that was done we had about two hours left to catch some sleep. Some couldn't sleep, some of us didn't bother. I was starting to get a little nervous but was really looking forward to the mission.

At 0210hrs on April 19 we had an early breakfast of hamburgers and coffee. Twenty minutes later Major Steve McCrohan, the rifle company commander, gave us our formal orders. One of my corporals, Nico, told me he had forgotten to load the schedule eight drugs, the major pain-relieving drugs like morphine and pethidine. After a couple of phone calls to wake the appropriate staff to unlock the drug safe, he was dispatched to the hospital to get the supplies. While he was gone, Major McCrohan put us in the picture about what was happening at Kibeho. The Rwandan Patriotic Army wanted the camp closed, and as quickly as possible. Major McCrohan said we might witness shooting in the distance or on a nearby hill, but that we were to take no notice. We were all to remain focused on the job at hand, and that was to supply medical support to the IDPs and the UN troops in the camp. The CCP would be protected by an infantry platoon led by Lieutenant Steve Tilbrook so that we could concentrate on our medical work. Although we were aware there was an element of danger, we were not expecting too much trouble. Ten minutes before we were due to leave at 0300hrs, I used the welfare phone to call Tara, who was eight days overdue. I was surprised to discover she had just gone into labour and her mother was driving her to the hospital. She wasn't impressed to find out I was heading south for a few days and there was no way she could contact me. She would have to pass any information on to my CSM, Scotty, who would radio me in the field. She wasn't happy, but I had my orders.

At 0300hrs, 32 people from the Australian medical support force (AMSF), consisting of five members of the CCP, two members of the evac team and a platoon of infantry for protection, departed Kigali in a convoy of six vehicles. I drove the CCP Land Rover with trailer. With me were Captain Carol Vaughan-Evans (doctor), Lieutenant Robbie Lucas (nursing officer), and Corporals Milan Nikolic and Tim Whyte (medical assistants) and an array of medical supplies. Also in the convoy were the evacuation team of two SAS patrol medics, Corporal Paul Jordan (Jordo) and Trooper Jon Church (Churchy), and their ambulance. Other personnel included two signallers, one staff sergeant and one signal operator Signalman Quinn, (Quinny). We also had one transport driver, one operations sergeant for liaison and an Intelligence Corps member, Corporal Tiddy. Major McCrohan joined us as the senior representative of the Australian Army.

After about five hours of driving through some of the roughest terrain in the country, we arrived at the Zambian Battalion (Zambatt) headquarters for a final briefing before travelling a further two hours to the Kibeho camp. As soon as we entered it was obvious that large areas had already been cleared, leaving thousands of makeshift shelters abandoned. Piles of personal belongings had been left behind and the whole area resembled a garbage dump. Many of the shelters had been burned down to stop the refugees returning. At first we thought the entire camp had already been emptied and that we had arrived too late. We continued on to the Zambatt Charlie Company position. As we entered, we drove through a sea of thousands and thousands of people who had been forced up to the area by the RPA. All the refugees cheered and clapped, thinking we had a lot to offer them and that we had come to protect them. I wondered what they expected a five-man CCP could do for 150,000 people. Some of our infantry had to walk in front of the vehicles just to clear a path for us to get through. There were so many faces jammed up against our vehicles it took a further 30 minutes to cover the last 400 metres. I have never seen anything like it in my life. This was truly a sea of humanity.

On arriving where we thought we needed to be, Major McCrohan made contact with the local RPA commander to find out where we could set up the CCP. While they talked the RPA officer excitedly waved his 9mm pistol – with the safety off and his finger on the trigger – in every direction which put us all a little on edge. In his other hand was a radio into which he would bark orders every now and then. The rest of us stood back, just in case the pistol was accidentally fired. Major McCrohan continued to speak with an air of authority, like it was no big deal, but I remember him saying later that he was a little nervous about that pistol being pointed at him. Eventually we set up the CCP in an abandoned building with all our electrical lifesaving equipment, generators, stretchers and trunks of medical stores laid out ready to get started. It took a good hour before we could tell the RPA officer we were ready for business. He then told us to pack up and move. He didn't want us there. We then tried to set up the Trelleborg inflatable tent but we were again ordered to move. As we packed our gear back onto the truck, some refugees began to help. While we waited for word as to where we were going, the staff sergeant signaller came sprinting across the compound to tell me that Tara had just given birth to a healthy baby girl. How strange it seemed that as I stood among all this desperation, my daughter had just been born halfway across the world.

After three hours of standing around we were told to move close to the RPA checkpoint about a kilometre further down the road. This was cordoned-off area of road where the refugees were searched, registered and then either put onto trucks for transporting back to their villages, or made to walk to Butare, about 20 kilometres away. Some were taken away for questioning by the RPA and were never seen again. We were to set up the CCP to work in conjunction with this checkpoint.

After much negotiation we were finally allocated a house to work from and got in by smashing down the door. Once our equipment was set up we advised the RPA that we were ready to begin treating anyone who needed it but they were not keen. Lieutenant Robbie Lucas and I, with small first aid kits over our shoulders, stood up on the road to identify sick or injured people as they streamed through the checkpoint. We were ready to guide them to the CCP for treatment, but the RPA refused to allow it. They thought it would delay the process of getting people through. In the end the only person we treated was a UN soldier. Baking in the heat and weighed down by our flak jackets, helmets, webbing and weapons, with little to do but make brews and cook our French rations, we all felt incredibly frustrated and disappointed.

It was considered too dangerous for us to be in Kibeho that night so we had to pack up everything and drive back to the Zambatt headquarters position at Cikongoro – a two-hour trip – where we could get some sleep. Stretchers were issued and we all grabbed what little space we could find. Our accommodation was a cramped, run-down building without any lighting. We ended up with about two square metres of space for each soldier – if we were lucky. We needed to cook our rations, clean our weapons and sort our own personal gear in this small space. Ablutions were outside, with bush toilet facilities and buckets of rainwater to wash with. I organised the restocking of medical supplies, water, fuel and rations. Some of the larger items of equipment – the inflatable tent, the generator and some of the electrical resuscitation equipment – were no longer necessary and I had them loaded onto another truck that we would leave there. One reason for doing this was some of the equipment was completely useless in the Kibeho environment. Another reason was to try and keep everyone busy so they didn't dwell on the day we'd had. Although there appeared to be no real danger in Kibeho, the mere sight of hundreds and hundreds of refugees, some of them injured, all of them very frightened, thirsty and hungry, being treated like sub-humans was daunting for us. We also knew some were being taken away for questioning by the RPA. We knew that they were in for a hard time and would probably be quietly killed.

That evening the Zambian RSM invited the signal staff sergeant and me to their sergeant's mess for some food. We both thought it had to be better than French rations and we were spot-on. It was also very spicy. When we asked for a drink of water the RSM took the glasses away from his own men and gave them to us which I found really embarrassing. The Zambian soldiers were extremely welcoming and went out of their way to accommodate us.

At 0600hrs the next morning we cooked our rations, made brews and followed our morning routine, using the Land Rover mirrors to shave. After a complete check of all equipment, vehicles and weapons, we set off for Kibeho and the house we had used the day before. Two sections of the infantry platoon joined us as protection, leaving one section behind to rest. When we arrived at the Zambatt Charlie Company position we were told by a Zambatt major that they were looking after a woman in one of their buildings who had just given birth. We were asked if our doctor could examine her because there was a problem. Captain Vaughan-Evans thought the woman could have a second unborn child still in her womb and since there were no heart sounds it was possibly dead. The woman needed urgent evacuation to Kigali by helicopter or she risked dying within 24 hours from septicemia as the undelivered child became gangrenous. The evacuation we could organise, but the problem was she wanted to take her two other children with her. After a sometimes heated discussion with other members of the CCP, I decided the children should go with another woman instead who had children of her own. It was unfair to expect the pilot to control two young children in a helicopter along with a sick mother and her newborn baby. The mother was moved to the landing zone and evacuated with her baby and we moved back to the house to again set up the CCP.

Carol tasked Robbie and me to stand on the road again to identify the sick and injured and to try to get some of them to the CCP for treatment. We took turns in the pouring rain as Lieutenant Tilbrook continued to negotiate with the RPA for permission. Eventually it was granted, but with a catch. We were only allowed to see people who would not hold up the checking process, with the RPA giving each patient a time limit of five minutes. Robbie and I sifted through the crowd walking towards us down the muddy road. I picked out people who had obvious wounds that were bleeding, or who were covered in bloody bandages and left the rest to pass by. Each patient had to be cleared by the RPA before going to the CCP. The RPA constantly checked up on us, often bursting through the front door without warning to make sure we were really doing medical work and not holding up patients for too long. Several times they simply came in and cleared all the patients out. It was a reminder of who was really the boss, and it was obviously not us. Sometimes the RPA would simply refuse to let a person be seen even though they were clearly injured. There was no particular rhyme or reason why. As I stood on the road I tried to talk to the RPA soldiers and get some sort of rapport going. *There is always tomorrow,* I thought, *and if I communicate with these soldiers now and be nice to them, try to get to know them a little then tomorrow they may let us see more injured or ill people.* I would just say things like, "The rain's a nuisance" or "It's really hot"; just keeping it as simple as possible. At times the refugees didn't understand I was trying to get them treatment for their wounds. All I could do was point to the red cross on my arm and then lead them to the CCP. They were worried that they might not be allowed to leave the camp or be taken away for questioning by the RPA. Later in the day I made a Red Cross flag out of a white bandage and a discarded little red dress. Today that flag is displayed in the School Of Army Health Museum at Bandiana in Victoria. When I wanted an injured refugee to get some treatment I pointed to my armband and then the flag and they got the message. But even then some would simply refuse to be seen. They just didn't want to be stopped or held up at the checkpoint. Fear was written all over their faces. They obviously knew more about what was happening in the refugee camp than we did, particularly at night when we were not there.

In between treating patients, we made sure we kept our fluid and food intake up. During the busy times we just shared around a water bottle. We all knew we had to keep our energy levels up to function properly, physically and mentally. We searched the house for anything we might be able to use and found suitcases of clothing which we used to dress some of the children we treated before sending them on their way. I found a small aluminum cup which I kept as a souvenir. I later had this mug engraved by the Ausmed dental assistant with all the names of the personnel who were at Kibeho during that horrific time. I only hope the next person who needed a filling didn't find the drill too blunt because there were 32 names!

Early in the afternoon we heard two bursts of automatic gun fire on the hill about 200 metres away. We asked the RPA about it and they told us that they had been only firing into the air to control the crowd. I recalled what Major McCrohan had said about staying focused on our work. None of us took any more notice. I was concerned there might be some stray rounds and we all made sure we had our flak jackets and helmets on and that our weapons were always at the ready. Not long after we received two patients, one with a fractured femur and another with a closed head injury. Both were stabilised and placed in the back of the ambulance. At about this time we all felt the tension in the air starting to build as the RPA began to show a real sense of urgency. They started wielding sticks and hitting people to try and speed them up through the checkpoint. The RPA were on the lookout for people they thought might be Interahamwe (gangs of people wanted for the genocide the previous year). More and more were being taken from the checkpoint for questioning. One suspect was a young boy wearing military-style pants. When asked where they came from, he replied, "From a dead person". He was escorted away and we never saw him again. Some of the refugees were simply dragged along the road if they didn't move quickly enough towards the checkpoint. A lot of the refugees lost all their belongings as the RPA took what they wanted. Bags of rice or flour, which was all the refugees had to live on, were thrown onto a pile behind the checkpoint. One poor man appeared determined to die rather than leave the camp. He was dragged along the road by four RPA soldiers. Each time they stopped he would leap up and run to the nearest vehicle and place his head under the front wheel, hoping to be run over and killed. He would then be knocked to the ground and dragged further down the road, his skin gradually being scrapped off his back.

Late in the afternoon we packed up all our medical supplies ready to leave for the night. While we waited at an RPA roadblock on the edge of the camp I heard several gunshots about 20 metres to my right. It made me extremely nervous. I badly wanted to get out and take up a good firing position as I had been trained to do, but in the end I chose simply to ignore it and proceeded through the roadblock as if nothing had happened. Once again my thoughts turned to Major McCrohan's instructions. On the way back to the Zambatt headquarters compound where we would once again safely spend the night, Jordo, Churchy, and Carol dropped the two patients they had in the ambulance at Butare hospital. That evening we again restocked and culled unnecessary equipment. I issued rations and made sure water bottles were refilled before cooking myself some dinner. The uniform I had worn for two days had become caked in mud and stained with blood. I washed it and hung it on a clothesline rigged between two vehicles. Refreshed by a good wash in a bucket of water, I slept solidly through the night without dreaming. What I didn't realise is that we would all confront a real nightmare during the next few days.

On Thursday April 20, after donning my still damp uniform, we returned to the Zambatt Charlie Company position at Kibeho. There the Zambian soldiers advised us that there had been killings during the night. Carol was asked to help check ten bodies left behind after a desperate attempt to get through the razor wire and into the Zambian compound. They were all children who had been either shot or trampled to death. There was nothing we could do for them so we moved on to our house near the RPA checkpoint and I took up my now familiar position on the road to triage the passing crowd. We saw little other evidence of killings during the night, but you could cut the tension with knife. The RPA was forcing refugees through the checkpoint, beating them with sticks and dragging them to make them hurry. Despite the RPA's reluctance to let us treat patients, we managed to help about 60. Many of them were children with bad flu. We gave them a handful of antibiotics and sent them on their way. Whenever the RPA were not looking we slipped the children our own rations and any clothing we could find in the abandoned house. As they'd done the previous day, the RPA occasionally came into the CCP and removed all our patients because we were taking too long. We treated a woman with a fractured femur and got her evacuated by air to Ausmed hospital in Kigali. I sent Nico as the AME medic even though he was not qualified because he had once worked at the Army School of Aviation in Oakey and probably had more knowledge than any of us about aero-medical evacuation.

Our public relations officer and his corporal set up a video camera and lights to film the work we were doing which made us very nervous. The RPA would not allow anyone to take photos, let alone footage. George Gittoes, the war artist attached to us, had been threatened with death if he took pictures. Instead, he hid his cameras in a bag with a small section cut out for the lens to poke through. He got some magnificent photos this way and many of them have been seen all over the world in magazine and television stories about Rwanda. As annoying as it was when he sometimes got in our way, I have to admit he had guts. He was determined to let the world know what was happening in Kibeho. He was also aware that his photos might be used one day to help bring some justice to the Rwandan people. I repeatedly asked the public relations major to stop filming. We were treating a couple of patients and I was finding it more and more difficult to keep an eye on the window at the same time in case any RPA soldiers were approaching. I finally yelled at him to stop and pack his gear up. He did so reluctantly and, unbelievably, about two minutes later the RPA came bursting through the door to check on the patients. Had he still been filming I have no doubt the situation could have got nasty. Weeks later, while on stand down in Nairobi, the major thanked me for stopping him that day. It could have been disastrous for all of us and he knew it.

Two patients, one of them with a sucking chest wound, needed immediate evacuation by road to Butare hospital. Carol and Churchy travelled in the back of the ambulance as Jordo drove and negotiated their way through RPA roadblocks and checkpoints. That evening, when the ambulance returned to Zambatt headquarters compound, it took Jordo and Churchy a good hour to clean out the blood and medical rubbish in preparation for the next day's work.

Throughout the next day there was sporadic gunfire on the same nearby hill. All the refugees were being herded into an area of about two square kilometres and there were tens of thousands of them. As we left that afternoon we could hear heavy bursts of automatic gunfire from AK47s in an area between two buildings that we knew as "the compound". We were all getting used to the sound and were not taking as much notice of it because at that stage none of it was being directed at us. The RPA maintained it was simply crowd control, but I was starting to wonder how much firing was needed to control a crowd of desperate, starving, unarmed and thirsty refugees. There had to be killings going on.

On Friday April 22, we returned to Kibeho. It was like a re-run of the morning before, only worse. The Zambian company commander informed us there had been many killings during the night. A representative from Medecins Sans Frontieres (Doctors without Borders), an international medical and humanitarian aid organisation, had a small set-up in one of the buildings next to the compound. He came to Carol and informed her that their facility had been inundated with casualties and they couldn't cope. Could we help in any way? Carol's answer had to be yes. I immediately tasked both Tim and Nico to start getting some of medical stores off the truck while Carol, Robbie, Jordo, Churchy and I went to the makeshift ward. After lengthy negotiations between the RPA and Lieutenant Tilbrook we were finally able to enter the building. The RPA really didn't want us getting too involved.

We went to the MSF ward to assess the situation for ourselves. It was horrific. The room was full of people with all sorts of terrible injuries. Some refugees were dead, others had shocking wounds caused by machete attacks and bullets. There were men, women and children ranging in age from just a few days to over 60. The floor was covered in blood and human waste. The stench was unbelievable. There was no toilet facilities, so raw sewage had soaked through the pieces of foam being used as mattresses and overflowed onto the floor. Taking little notice of the situation they were in – or perhaps because they used to it – the people who could were cooking over little fires in the middle of the floor and eating the food. Some of the children were picking the corn out of the human waste lying around the floor and eating it. Some of the mothers did the same, but first re-cooked the corn in tins of water heated over their little fires. The RPA had cut off all food and water supplies to the camp five days earlier. Now the refugees were showing their sheer desperation to survive. I thought I knew all about survival in harsh situations. I was a survival instructor for the Army. But to see people being forcibly lowered to this level was extremely distressing. It was an absolutely awful thing to witness – the complete degradation of human beings. And I was absolutely stunned.

Each of us started to treat a casualty. I bandaged up a girl with some horrific cuts to her arms. But after a few minutes of looking around it became very obvious that to continue in these circumstances would only be disastrous. What we had to do was assess the whole area, not just one makeshift ward, or we would lose more people by not treating them in the correct order. Carol decided that we all should go back to our vehicles, leaving Jordo and Churchy and Robbie Lucas to triage in this ward. Lieutenant Tilbrook left some of the infantry soldiers as security for Jordo and Churchy and also tasked them to act stretcher-bearers if required.

At our vehicles Lieutenant Tilbrook asked Carol if she wanted to call in a "mass casualty situation" to Australian headquarters. After considering all the options, she did so. This would allow our headquarters in Kigali to put plans into action to evacuate a large number of casualties. This would mean placing surgical teams on standby and recalling all medical staff to duty. The UN would also provide helicopters for aero-medical evacuation. Poor Quinny, the signaller, was going to be working flat-out sending and receiving messages to and from Kigali for the rest of the time we were in the camp. With that we started to treat the casualties brought into the CCP, all of them having been stretchered from the makeshift ward by the infantry teams.

Meanwhile, Churchy and Jordo decided it was no longer feasible to work in the MSF ward because as fast as they treated someone and moved them out, another casualty arrived. Most had horrific machete wounds and the blood was fresh. Ominously, it meant that they were being attacked right there and then, just around the corner. As the number of injured got larger, Jordo and Churchy decided it was safer to leave the MSF ward and join us at the CCP to help treat the people who had come to us.

The tension was reaching boiling point as we dealt with a disturbing range of injuries from sucking chest wounds to open fractures and very deep lacerations. Every single casualty had been shot or attacked with machetes. One of the first I treated that day was a man, approximately 40 years old. I conducted my primary survey on him and all seemed well. He was fully conscious and orientated and had a strong heartbeat. While conducting my secondary survey I found a small entry wound caused by a bullet in the centre of his chest. There was no exit wound. I dressed the wound as I normally would since he appeared to have no difficulty breathing. Like all the refugees, he was very dehydrated. I put up a drip of 4% glucose—1/5 sodium and got this flowing. As I kept an eye on him I noticed that he was starting to deteriorate rapidly. His level of consciousness lowered and his pulse became very irregular. Knowing that he would be in pain, I gave him about seven milligrams of morphine intravenously, quickly calculating one milligram per 10 kilograms of body weight. I forgot that this person would be lucky to weigh 40 kilograms in the state he was in. He kept getting worse so I got Carol involved. She did a quick check on him and advised me that he was going to die. We could only deduce that the round had ruptured his aorta and the drip had increased his circulating blood volume. This had increased the internal bleeding and there was bugger all I could do about it. With more morphine on board than he really needed, his respiratory system had slowed down as well. Carol had more casualties to see so she told me just to stay with this man. I sat with him, gently held his hand and talked in a soft voice. I remembered reading somewhere that a person's hearing is thought to be the last sense to go, so I kept talking as his pulse gradually slowed and finally ceased. I said goodbye to him, closed his eyes and had him moved to an area out of the way. It was time for me to treat the next casualty.

Later Carol suggested to me that we should remove any Australian medical material from this man. The reason was we did not want the RPA, in their twisted way, blaming us for causing his death and then using it as an excuse to retaliate in some way. I found his body, which had been moved into the gutter, and removed all the bandaging and dressings that I had applied. Lastly, I removed the drip. I apologised to him and covered his face with his own shirt. I left him in the gutter because there was nowhere else to put him. His body was later taken away by the Zambatt soldiers and buried in one of the mass graves that were starting to appear around the area. I felt terrible for that man but I couldn't dwell on him for long. The number of casualties was rapidly increasing. I had to push all my emotions out of my mind and get working on the next patient.

As the tension between the RPA and the refugees worsened by the minute, it brought another threatening development. The RPA would enter the ward and clear people out using sticks. They said anyone who did not leave could be shot and they meant what they said. Occasionally when we were away from the ward we would hear gunshots. The next time we entered the ward somebody was missing or there was someone else lying badly injured with gunshot wounds. Some who had been alive when we left the ward were now dead. Lieutenant Tilbrook would sometimes not allow us back into the MSF hospital to pick up more casualties because he thought it was not safe to enter. He was repeatedly forced to negotiate for us to go in and get more casualties out for treatment. He did this over and over again, for the whole day. Only when he read the situation as relatively safe would he allow us in, and then only with an infantry escort.

Two stretchers and an Oxyviva machine used to administer oxygen had been left behind in the rush to get out of the MSF ward. When our only other machine in the CCP broke down I was unable to repair it. We needed to get the other one back. I got permission from Lieutenant Tilbrook for me and two infantry soldiers to return to the MSF ward to try and retrieve the equipment. An RPA officer refused to let us in so I asked for the stretchers and machine to be returned. We got the stretchers back, but not the Oxyviva. He told us to leave but I started to argue that we needed it to treat some of the casualties. When about a platoon of RPA arrived, I decided that it was not worth endangering our lives to push it any further. We returned to the CCP with the two stretchers and no Oxyviva. The machines were worth more than $2,000 apiece and I had to get that one written off when I later returned to Kigali. As we continued to work on about 30 casualties, Jordo, Churchy and some soldiers would return to the MSF ward to try and retrieve more injured. The casualties were ferried on stretchers or simply carried in the arms of the soldiers. George Gittoes managed to get a photo of Churchy carrying a small child towards our CCP position which was later used on army recruiting posters and a postage stamp.

At about 1000hrs we had around about 20 casualties lined up against the brick wall where the CCP was set up. All hell broke loose around us. There was an immense amount of gunfire very close to us. I had no idea what the hell was going on. I didn't know whether to go to ground and adopt a defensive fire position as I was trained to do or continue treating the casualty I was working on. I was on my knees, with my weapon at the ready, having a quick look around when Jordo ran into our position and told us we were right to continue working. He had checked and found that all of our own infantry and a couple of Zambatt soldiers had formed a defensive ring on the wire all around us, so we were completely covered from all sides. I picked myself up and continued treating my patient. He had suffered an open fracture to the left humerus (upper arm) with arterial bleeding. I felt confident that we were relatively safe against the brick wall and with our own boys out there on the wire so we all got on with our work.

The gunfire intensified until it was almost continuous. During small breaks in the firing Lieutenant Tilbrook negotiated with the RPA for permission for teams to reenter the MSF ward to extract more casualties. We would move in quickly and remove as many as possible before the lieutenant called a halt. Then the gunfire would start again. Our soldiers had many close calls as someone took pot shots at them. We had no idea when the firing would start or where it would come from. We returned to the CCP area to begin treatment. The radio operator, Quinny, started sending casevac requests to headquarters back in Kigali. As I positioned the treated casualties in an evacuation area, I simply shouted the information he needed over the top of all the noise. This included what priority I had allocated to each of them, the types of injuries suffered and the mode of transport required to get them out. One set of figures I gave him was five priority one, seven priority two, and thirteen priority three. Priority one was the most severely injured. The figures changed very quickly as I altered the priority of one casualty, or more injured refugees were added. Then I just yelled out the updated figures to Quinny and he transmitted the information back to headquarters.

With so much medical work going on, all our equipment began to weigh on us. It was getting really hot and uncomfortable. Sweat ran down the inside of my helmet, stinging my eyes and soaking my body and uniform under the flak jacket. If someone had time to stop and have a drink, they would pass the water bottle around for everyone else. The sick and injured were all badly dehydrated and desperate for water. I got everyone to mark the lid of one of their water bottles with a black pen. From then on the bottle was only to be used for casualties to ensure we did not pick up any diseases like dysentery, hepatitis or cholera which were no doubt flourishing in such a filthy environment.

We treated people all day as the shooting continued around us. Occasionally a round landed nearby, kicking up dust or smacking into the wall, but gradually we became more immune to it all. We weren't blasé about it. We were very aware of the danger, but when you are trying to help so many casualties and to keep so many alive, things like gunfire seem to become part of the background as you just get on with what you are doing. Our situation was complicated by the number of young children coming to us for sanctuary. They had been told by their mothers that if anything bad happened they should go to where the white men were. Only some made it to the compound where we treated them. I saw Jordo yelling and waving at one child who was confused about which way to go. Jordo was trying to get this boy to come to us but he was so scared that he froze. With so many rounds flying around he would not have lasted long. It was then that I saw Jordo do the most amazing and bravest thing I have ever witnessed. He ran to the boy, who was stuck in an area under intense fire, grabbed him in both arms and ran back to us. Jordo put the boy in the back of the truck where Nico was looking after several refugees awaiting evacuation to the landing zone. He then went back to the patient he had been treating as if nothing had happened.

A minute later the boy fell off the back of the truck. Nico said we should leave him because he was dead, but Jordo was adamant he couldn't be dead because he had just saved him. When I looked at the boy I saw him move. Jordo and I started to work on him before Carol took over. The boy had suffered some shrapnel wounds to his chest. It wasn't clear whether he was injured before or after Jordo rescued him, but I believe it happened while he was on the back of the truck.

Quinny passed a message to me from Ausmed that three evacuation helicopters would be arriving to take our casualties out, so I commandeered a Zambatt truck and driver to take some of them to the landing zone 200—300 metres away. I put the worst of the priority one casualties in the ambulance and squeezed the rest into the back of the truck. There must have been at least thirty wounded, each with a drip, crammed into the truck with Nico – the only medic to look after them. The choppers were not due for a while so the truck had to remain at the ready. One of the infantry diggers asked if he could help. I asked if he could do basic bandaging. When he said yes, I gave him a heap of roller bandages and told him to bandage the elbow over there, then the head around the corner and then anything else he could find. It was then that I realised the casualties had ceased to be casualties to me. In my mind they had become just a series of injuries. I had begun to dehumanise these people. It was one of the ways I coped with the overwhelming amount of horrifically wounded we were faced with.

Another infantry soldier wanted to help so I commandeered another truck and filled it with priority three patients who were not in immediate danger. I gave him the "soldier's five" on how to look after bags of fluid on the drips. I showed him how to change the bag when it ran out and got him to then show me so I knew he could do it. I asked if he felt confident doing it alone and left him to it when he said yes. This freed up the medical team to focus on the more seriously wounded. Another soldier decided he needed a break and picked out a quiet area where he cooked himself a very large brew of coffee.

Noticing that none of us had time to make coffee or get some food, he shared his brew with us in good Aussie fashion. He handed it to Carol, who had some and then handed it on. To his amazement, it quickly disappeared as it made the rounds of the medics. All he got back was his empty cups canteen.

At about 1200hrs we began moving some of the casualties by ambulance to the landing zone (LZ). The chopper brought some of the medical stores that I had requested earlier, including a new Oxyviva and some stretchers. Jordo and I managed to fit nine priority ones and two other casualties on board. When all the injured were secured, we noticed a pool of blood forming under the seating. We looked at each other and shook our heads. The blood was pouring out of one casualty with abdominal injuries. There was no way we were going to tell the pilot because he would not take them, so we just carried on like nothing was wrong. I again sent Nico on the flight as the medic. He was carrying about 15 rolls of film that had been given to me by the public relations major, who told me it was vital that we get them back to Australian headquarters in Kigali. I put them in an empty ammunition pouch and told Nico to wear it on his webbing. When I told him what it was he said that there was no way he would take it. We all knew the RPA's policy on photos and Nico was really nervous about getting caught. In the end I had to say, "That is an order, corporal". I figured that an extra ammo pouch would not attract any attention. It didn't. After the helicopter took off, Jordo and I returned to the CCP area. We were surprised to see it return thirty minutes later and I realised they had gone to Butare and not Kigali. The chopper had to shut down so it could be reconfigured to take our laying casualties. Nico, with a big smile, gave me back the ammo pouch of film. He was glad to get rid of it. I had no idea what to do with it. I couldn't give it to a patient and nobody else was going back to Kigali, so I attached it to my webbing.

The casualty count was mounting quickly, forcing us to treat people faster. Medical stores were getting so low we had to use the same cannula (tube) on a patient more than once. We ran out of alcohol swabs and had to resort to using water to clean patients and our hands. Gloves were not changed but just washed between casualties. Some of the old bandages were removed from the dead and reused on the living. In desperation we began to conserve as many supplies as possible to enable us to treat as many as possible. The situation was becoming dire. We had to do our best with what we had and that was bugger all. We continued to treat quite a large number of casualties up against the wall – about the safest position we could find. Tim was at one end, with Carol, Robbie and me at the other. It had been raining for a while.

When we ran out of water to wash our hands, Jordo lowered the back hatch of the ambulance and used the rainwater that had collected to refill the bucket. Now we were really desperate. It felt like we were living in a nightmare.

We started to see a lot more horrifically injured children and this played on Robbie's mind. He was having trouble with some tasks so Carol and I got him to do some less confrontational things like fetching blankets and water. I could see Robbie had reached his limit and I spoke quietly to Carol about it. We all handle things differently. Robbie had two kids of his own and was badly affected by what was happening to the children around us. I got him to go with the worst of the priority one casualties on the reconfigured chopper because I knew it was definitely going back to Kigali. As he boarded the chopper I remembered the film. I handed him the ammo pouch and told him to make sure he got it back to Ausmed headquarters. He ended up performing CPR on one of the patients for most of the flight back to Kigali.

With Robbie gone our team was down one medic and we all had to work that little bit harder. The firing was slowly becoming more intense and we could hear the rounds whizzing past us. How none of us got hit still amazes me. I dispatched one of the trucks with priority three casualties off to Butare with one of the Zambatt medics as an escort which helped reduce our casualty count. With the next choppers due at 1500hrs, Lieutenant Tilbrook began negotiating with the RPA to let us get the wounded to the LZ and we were finally able to send the ambulance with the worst of the laying casualties. Jordo looked after that while I followed on foot behind another truck full of casualties with Nico in the back looking after about thirty people, which he had done for the past three hours. On the slow, bumpy drive towards the LZ one of the RPA soldiers decided he would stop the truck with the idea of getting into the back to check the casualties and make sure we were not trying to smuggle people out. We just wanted to get to the LZ as quickly as possible so we could unload the casualties and get them out of here. By this stage Nico had had a gutful. Fuming at the way the RPA soldier demanded to check our patients, Nico yelled at him to "Fuck off". *Now we're in for it*, I thought. With our infantry still securing the CCP area and the LZ, we were by ourselves. I ended up between them, trying to explain to the RPA soldier that all we had were injured people. At the same time I was trying to calm Nico down. I told him to "Shut the fuck up" and let the soldier get on the truck and do what he had to do. As soon as he had finished trying to show us that he was in charge, he let us pass and carry on to the LZ. Nico gave him the finger. Luckily it meant nothing to him.

The first chopper arrived and with Jordo's help we managed to get seven wounded on board. With a one-hour wait until the next chopper, Nico and I were forced to stay at the LZ with our truck of injured while Jordo and Churchy returned to the CCP area to get more priority one casualties ready. Feeling really exposed out in the open on the LZ, we talked during lulls in the firing about what we would do when we all got back to our barracks in Kigali. Having a beer was high on the list. Jordo and Churchy returned with another ambulance load and the RPA again decided to check the truck. About a dozen of them headed our way, but none were keen on staying long after firing broke out near us. Apparently there was a sniper in the building of the compound we had just left taking pot shots at both the RPA and us. The refugees would panic and start running towards the LZ, prompting the RPA to open fire again to try and control them. The sniper would then fire a few rounds to make the people panic again, and the RPA would respond again by opening fire. The problem was that we were in the middle of it. Some of the rounds were landing in the LZ – two grazed the ambulance – and there was absolutely nothing we could do about it. All we could do was stay as low to the ground as possible, grit our teeth, hope nothing would happen to us and wait. Some of the tension I was feeling only eased when one of our infantry sections came down to the LZ during a lull in the firing and formed a secure perimeter around us.

None of the pilots were keen on trying to land a chopper in the middle of firing but the next one came in safely. On board were Scotty, the medical company CSM, and Sergeant Brett Dick. We squeezed in as many sitting casualties as we could and the chopper was dispatched to Butare with Brett as escort. A short time later it returned but then had to shut down to reconfigure so that it could take laying casualties. Feeling exposed to the firing going on all around, I began to get frustrated by the wait and yelled to the CSM to "Hurry the fuck up" so we could get out of there. He just calmly told me to be quiet and settle down a bit. I was fuming. He had only just arrived so he was not fully aware of what we had all been through in the last few days. Angry and apprehensive, I sat on the LZ, putting myself between my laying casualty and the carnage going on around us. Even though some rounds were still landing near, I hardly cared. I just sat there for ten minutes which gave me time to cool off and get myself together. Finally we got the rest of the casualties on board and we prepared to head back to the compound.

Little did I know I was about to descend a lot further into hell.

Chapter Five

Worse than hell

"An old lady near us stood up and raised her hands in surrender. A RPA soldier went to her and escorted her to the top of the hill. That's good, I thought, she will be safe now. But then, to our horror, the soldier turned around, looked at us with a big smile on his face, pushed the old woman to the ground and shot her in the back."

After loading the last of the priority one casualties onto the helicopter, we needed to get back to the safety of the Zambatt compound; and fairly quickly by the sound of things. The sound of sporadic RPA shooting was coming from all directions as the situation deteriorated rapidly. About 15 of us managed to squeeze into the back of the ambulance. While climbing in it occurred to me that sitting anywhere near the middle was a bad idea because it was directly in line with the large red cross painted on the outside of the vehicle. That red cross was an excellent aiming mark and I wanted to be as far away from it as possible. I also wanted to be able to exit quickly if I had to, so I parked myself near the rear door. Scotty, Churchy and Jordo followed on foot. When we arrived at the Zambatt compound one of our soldiers flung open the door and yelled for everyone to get out, keep low and get to the safety of the nearest sandbag bunkers. Since everyone seemed to be heading left, I headed right. I didn't want to end up in a bunker with so many soldiers that I had little chance of being protected. Jordo held the door open until all of us were out safely. Churchy crouched down to keep a watchful eye on our surroundings. Then they followed me.

Keeping me company in the same sandbag bunker were Scotty, Carol, Jordo, Churchy, Lieutenant Tilbrook, a UN observer with his binoculars and a Zambatt corporal. As we crouched down, one of the infantry section corporals would occasionally join us with his handheld radio to keep Lieutenant Tilbrook updated. With so many people behind such an unimposing sandbag wall, it wasn't long before Carol headed for another bunker and Lieutenant Tilbrook and his corporal to another. The UN observer also moved off, leaving me with Churchy, Jordo, Scotty and the Zambatt corporal. I had no idea where the rest of the Zambian soldiers were.

Meanwhile at the LZ the last evacuation chopper was starting to wind up for takeoff. Sergeant Brett Dick, a qualified AME (air medical evacuation) medic, had to hold the chopper's main rotor while the pilot got the motors started. Despite the shooting, Brett continued to stand out in the open for around five minutes to help the pilot. I watched, hoping that nothing would happen to them until finally the chopper was ready for takeoff. The pilot, deciding that he needed to take off as quickly as possible, got airborne with only one jet at full power. Brett jumped aboard and they flew down the valley until the second jet kicked in, enabling them to rise to a safe height. As they headed for Butare the pilot told Brett to listen out for any pinging sounds. "What would that mean," asked Brett. The pilot told him it would mean the aircraft was being hit by gunfire. Luckily, Brett didn't hear anything. The immense amount of weapons firing in the Kibeho camp meant that helicopter didn't return.

We later learnt that while we were at the LZ loading our casualties onto the choppers, the RPA commanders in the church building had got their soldiers so wound up that by the time they emerged they were chanting and primed to take action. To some they appeared as they were in a different state of mind. They were ready to kill anything. And they had been ordered not to let any of the refugees leave the camp. They believed that some of the Interahamwe responsible for the genocide of 1994 could be among the IDPs, so the soldiers were not going to let any of them escape among the innocent. The RPA's solution was to kill any IDPs trying to break through the ring of soldiers. Back at our bunker all hell was breaking loose around us. Some of the refugees had panicked and started running towards the checkpoint to try and get out. That was when the RPA opened fire with AK47s and rocket-propelled grenades. They also had a 50-calibre machinegun pumping away on the nearby hill overlooking the checkpoint. We could see the RPGs wobbling through the air as they headed for their target and landing among groups of refugees, killing up to half. The survivors were then mown down with rifle and machinegun fire. We could only sit and watch in horror. The restrictions placed on us by the UN charter meant we weren't allowed to react in any way with our own weapons. Under our rules of engagement, we couldn't act because our own lives were not being directly threatened. The UN had ordered us not to intervene; this was a local matter that needed to be sorted out by the Rwandan people themselves. It was all very well for them to give those orders, but they were not on the ground like we were. I felt helpless as I knelt behind the sandbag wall and watched person after person get slaughtered. For the first time in my life, I wanted to use my rifle to kill someone. But I have no doubt that if any of us had killed one of the RPA soldiers, or even fired our weapons, we would have been wiped out. As Jordo said years later in an interview for Channel 9's *Sunday* programme, "We were good, but not that good". There were around 2,000 RPA soldiers, all focused on killing, and only 32 of us. I have no doubt their numerical advantage would have overwhelmed us and we would have been wiped out.

The RPA continually tried to intimidate and provoke us. They were just looking for the chance to start shooting at us, waiting for one of us to fire at them. Only our discipline as Australian soldiers stopped us. One incident sticks in my memory. An old lady near us stood up and raised her hands in surrender. A RPA soldier went to her and escorted her to the top of the hill. *That's good*, I thought, *she will be safe now*. But then, to our horror, the soldier turned around, looked at us with a big smile on his face, pushed the old woman to the ground and shot her in the back. I have no doubt he did this deliberately, as if to say, "The UN is not in control here. I am." Basically, he was giving us the big finger and daring us to do something about it. We couldn't do anything at all. And he knew it. They all knew it.

A minute or so later, three refugees came running over the hill directly to the front of our bunker. No more than 20 metres away, they had the widest, panic-stricken eyes I have ever seen. They were trying to get to the apparent safety of the UN compound. They knew they would be killed if they couldn't find protection. But there was none. They were close to us when I said to the others that we had better get our heads below the level of the sandbags because I knew they would make attractive targets to the RPA. We all ducked down and within a few seconds a massive amount of automatic machinegun and rifle fire was directed into the area. When the shooting died down and we looked up, all three were dead. It was a man, woman and child; most likely a family. The look of pure desperation and animal-like fear in the father's dark, wide eyes will be burned into my memory forever.

It was at this time that I think my mind started to try and find ways to cope with the horror of what was playing out in front of me. The reality of what had become an extremely desperate, horrific and dangerous situation was simply too much for me to take in. And rather than go to pieces, I resorted to a kind of black humour which someone who wasn't there, or who has never faced a similar situation, simply would not understand. Churchy and I started estimating how long we thought a particular running refugee would live. I would say, "About a minute", and Churchy would estimate 20 seconds. He was usually right. Most only lasted about 30 seconds before being cut down by a hail of bullets. We did this for a while, identifying people in the distance by the colour of their shirts. We would count the seconds until the person fell and then pick another coloured shirt and start counting again. We soon tired of it and ended up just watching the slaughter quietly, waiting for it to end as we sat behind our meagre sandbag wall. That is all we were – observers.

Occasionally a round would land near our position, just to remind us of danger we were in. One of the Interahamwe snipers from somewhere in the building would fire the odd shot at us to try and provoke us into returning fire. I think they hoped it would cause the RPA to then fire at us, creating confusion which would allow the Interahamwe to slip out of the camp. We never gave them the pleasure, but it was certainly very tempting. The weather began to deteriorate and rain started to sweep across the valley when suddenly the Zambatt corporal got up and ran to the nearby building. *This is just great,* I thought, *where the fuck is he off to?* If we had to defend our position, Jordo, Churchy, Scotty and I had our Steyrs. I knew the other three had pistols under their flak jackets and between us we probably had about 200—300 rounds of ammunition. But the Zambatt corporal's departure meant we had just lost our only machinegun, a Minimi, and several belts of ammo. I was starting to get really anxious about whether we had enough firepower to defend ourselves if the shit hit the fan. I knew we would give it our best shot but the numbers were against us. To my great relief, a couple of minutes later the Zambatt corporal reappeared with his light machinegun and knelt back down behind the wall. He had only gone to get his raincoat. Some of my confidence returned but I seriously hoped we wouldn't have to defend ourselves.

Meanwhile, the killing just went on and on right in front of us. Those who were unfortunate enough not to be killed outright lay injured in the field until they were hunted down and shot at close range. Some were simply bayoneted were they lay, so the RPA could conserve ammunition. None were spared, not even the babies on their mother's backs. Many had their throats cut. The things I saw through my Steyr's telescopic sight were almost impossible to comprehend. When a machinegun is fired it tends to leave a pattern where the rounds land called the "beaten zone". Rounds do not land in exactly the same spot and have a spray effect. I had seen this many times on the range in Australia. I had never seen the effect when humans were the target. I had a close-up view of people dropping to the ground as they were hit. As shocking as it sounds, it went on for so long a kind of boredom set in. After a while I got talking to the Zambian soldier crouching next to me. I asked him what he thought of the RPA and what they were doing to the refugees. I wanted to know his opinion as someone from Africa. He explained to me that he thought the RPA were not people but animals with the ability to use weapons. He also reminded me that these two tribes, the Hutu and the Tutsi, had been at each other's throats for many, many generations. The only difference now was they used AK47s and machineguns instead of spears and shields.

As I sat there I came to the sudden and horrible conclusion that none of us were going to live out the day. I figured that we were witnessing a massacre on a massive scale and the RPA would not want the world to know. For their government, it could mean UN sanctions and more reprisals from other countries. I believed that when all the refugees were killed we would be disposed of as well. Nearly 800,000 people had been killed in Rwanda, so what would stop them now? There were only 32 of us and they could always use the excuse that we had opened fire. Who would know? It was raining heavily, so I thought, *fuck, I am going to get my raincoat.* The rain was really teeming down and we were all getting soaked. I just stood up and walked through the mud and puddles, with no concern for my own safety, to the building where my pack was. I removed my webbing, placed my weapon on the ground, dragged the raincoat out, put it on over my flak jacket, replaced my webbing, picked up my weapon and then just walked back to the bunker. I was aware that this was a very stupid thing to do, but right at that particular moment I did not give a fuck because I thought we were all going to die anyway. What was the point? Well, as I sat back down behind the sandbags it became clear to me. I looked at the others and tried to summon up all of my personal strength and discipline to force these negative thoughts out of my mind. I needed to focus on our ability as Australians to get out of this situation. I struggled to get some control of myself. After a couple of minutes I got it together again and started feeling much better. I could not afford any negative thoughts. I was an Australian soldier, a sergeant and a medic, and I still had a job to do. My mates around me might have to depend on me. There was no way I was going to let them down, or myself. I thought back to the Anzacs and the defiant spirit they had shown, and then thought of all the great things Australian soldiers had done all over the world. I was proud to be Australian, and no matter what was happening I knew I could not afford to let it stop me doing my job.

As the rain sweeping across the valley increased in intensity the firing began to abate. After a while we felt it was safe enough to stand up and move away from the spot we had crouched in for the past couple of hours. We now had to get ourselves and all our gear packed onto our vehicles and then, we hoped, leave this place safely. We started to gather what was left of our supplies and gear. We looked around at the hundreds of dead scattered on the ground to the front of our position. We could hear the injured crying out in pain. There was nothing more we could do this day to help these people. We had to get out while it was still daylight. And we could only hope the RPA would allow us to leave after what we had witnessed. What had just happened would become known as the "Kibeho Massacre". Would the RPA allow witnesses to this atrocity leave the camp and tell the world about it? Or were they going to wipe us out as well? We would just have to wait and see. With Scotty beside me in the Land Rover, both of us soaking wet, the heater on full blast, we started to head out of Kibeho in convoy for Gikongoro. Accompanying us were all the NGO vehicles and their staff, their vehicles interspersed with our own. It was the only safe way for them to leave since they weren't armed. We had to pass through checkpoint after checkpoint, with Lieutenant Tilbrook negotiating our way at each one. Although we had been given permission to leave the camp by one of the senior RPA officers, there was no communication between the checkpoints so we were forced to stop every time. At the first one virtually every vehicle was searched and we waited hours to proceed. It was our first chance all day to eat and we opened our French ration packs, passing them along the convoy to share with the NGO staff. There was a lot of small talk as everyone's thoughts turned to getting out of there and back to the safety of the Zambatt night location. It was a nerve-jangling wait, but eventually we got moving.

After clearing the roadblocks we pushed on to the Zambatt Bravo Coy position where we would stay the night. The NGOs headed off to their own destinations as we continued in our convoy. I was driving the Land Rover and trailer behind Lieutenant Tilbrook's vehicle when he went left at one of the turnoffs. I didn't see him in the dark and missed the turn. We drove another three kilometres before I realised what had happened and did a U-turn and headed back the way we'd come. I almost ran into Lieutenant Tilbrook's vehicle as he came looking for us. He got out and told me I should have known the way back by now considering we had made the trip several times. This made me angry because I had always followed other vehicles in convoy, so how would I know the way back? It wasn't my job to navigate. We had a few heated words before Scotty settled us both down and we continued on. I guess we were stressed and little things were starting to really get to us.

After arriving and securing the vehicle I ran into Brett Dick. He asked me what had happened and without thinking I snapped that if he had walked in a big puddle of mud right here and right now and got his boots really dirty then he would be the same as us. What I was trying to say was if he got dirty he might feel the way we were after what we had witnessed. I still had a lot of adrenalin running through my body. Straight away I regretted saying it and apologised. I felt like a right dickhead. How was he to know what we had been through? I quickly told him my version of what happened and he told me what he had seen from the chopper.

Inside the building George Gittoes wanted to take some group photos, starting with the infantry sections. Believing that history would have more to say about Kibeho, he felt it was important to have a photographic record of who was involved. Most of us were exhausted and some of the soldiers just sat there feeling quite numb. When it was the CCP's turn to have their photo taken, I put my flak jacket and webbing on and held my weapon. Carol asked if I was going to wear all of it and I replied, "Why the fuck not, I had to wear it all day". So the four of us put on all of our gear, held onto our weapons and had our photo taken. I held the homemade Red Cross flag in front of us. When it was Jordo and Churchy's turn as members of the evacuation section, they followed our lead. Despite our exhaustion, there was still a lot to do. I made sure my team got something to eat and drink before I used the radio to send another operational demand (OPDEM) for replacement medical stores to headquarters. We barely had anything left. Sending a long OPDEM over the radio is trying because you have to stop and get confirmation from the other end. Medical terminology can be hard enough to understand at the best of times, but it's even harder for non-medical personnel over a radio. I managed to get the message across but it was difficult after such a life-changing day.

The next thing to tackle was a brew and some food. I was so hungry I managed to eat a whole French ration pack which is no mean feat. I sat with Tim and Nico, and both of them seemed fine. It was good to be able to sit with the people who had been with me through the whole episode. We were all able to talk freely about things that we saw or felt. To others the things we said might have sounded unbelievable, but we knew what we had seen. We knew it was true. Somehow we managed to laugh about a few things. I guess it was a way to release tension. Carol briefed the new CCP doctor on what to expect the next day before briefing the rest of the new CCP. Lieutenant Tilbrook briefed the replacement infantry platoon commander. The adrenalin had left us feeling really hyped-up, so even though we were exhausted we went to sleep very late that night.

The next morning we began to ready ourselves for another day at Kibeho. As I shaved with the help of the Land Rover mirror, Nico told me he might not bother with the razor that day because there was really no point. Stunned, I immediately got stuck into him, reminding him he was a corporal and he should be setting an example to the other soldiers. I gave him my razor and cup of water and told him to shave. In my mind I believed I needed to nip this apparent loss of discipline in the bud right then and there. I had to have corporals, particularly medics, who could do their job and still work well under pressure which all of us had done so far. Once you start to let a little lack of discipline go by, it doesn't take long for it to become a big problem. We certainly didn't need that heading into Kibeho for another day.

Chapter Six

Aftermath

" Jordo and Scotty had already counted about 4,000 dead and 650 wounded when they were stopped halfway along the road. The RPA had forced them to stop when they realised what was going on. There were bodies lying all over the place even though the RPA had tried to get rid of many of them during the night."

We returned to Kibeho early the next day accompanied by a second CCP team. On the long drive there I thought about what we were about to see. Most of us were quiet and, I think, a little nervous. I was mentally preparing myself for the worst. I knew I would see dead and injured, but I believed everything would be relatively settled. I assumed the dead would have been collected and buried and most of the injured removed and treated. I guess I was hoping the place would be deserted. Boy, how wrong I was! What confronted us was a picture of absolute disaster. Hundreds of bodies lay where they had fallen despite the RPA's efforts to remove truckloads during the night. The number of injured was incomprehensible and the types of injuries were incredibly varied. No matter where you looked it was a scene of utter devastation. The wailing and moaning of the injured was terrifying. The sight nearly blew my mind away. But I had a job to do and I just had to get on with it.

As soon as we arrived at the Zambatt Charlie Company position the corporals began setting up the CCP and Captain Carol Vaughan-Evans tasked Brett and I to negative triage the huge number of injured. That meant getting out the easiest casualties first and leaving the more complicated and difficult ones for later. It was the only way to get as many people treated in the quickest time and hopefully saving as many lives as possible. It also speeded up the evacuation for many of the injured. While Brett and I got started, Nico and Tim set up the CCP, which was basically a Unimog truck with tarpaulins tied off the sides. Trunks of medical stores were laid out beside the truck along with plenty of stretchers on which we could treat or evacuate the injured. The CCP's Land Rover and trailer were parked alongside, and held jerry cans of water and medical supplies left over from the day before. Nico and Tim constructed a large shaded treatment area as well as a second area that served as a holding bay where people would go after they were seen. From there they would be put on waiting trucks supplied by the Zambians for evacuation to Butare or Kigali. The ambulance would only be used to ferry the worst of the casualties to the LZ for helicopter evacuation.

Jordo and Scotty, each accompanied by an infantry section, were tasked to walk up the sides of the road to do a body count using pace counters. Jordo and Scotty had already counted about 4,000 dead and 650 wounded when they were stopped halfway along the road. The RPA had forced them to stop when they realised what was going on. There were bodies lying all over the place even though the RPA had tried to get rid of many of them during the night. While counting in the compound, Jordo and his section found a large number of dead women who still had young children tied to their backs in the

African way. Jordo had to go around and cut the children and babies free. Some were already dead. Others had been forced to spend the whole night nestled against their dead mothers. The children who were still alive were carefully collected by the Zambatt soldiers and taken to the water point to be registered before being loaded onto trucks bound for orphanages around the country. The dead were thrown into mass graves.

Brett and I started moving around the MSF ward and the compound next to it to triage the casualties. Our main problem was where to start. The sheer number of injured and dead seemed overwhelming. We walked the whole area to find out what we were up against. Everywhere we looked, in every room and area, there were horrifically injured people. With some of the infantry soldiers acting as stretcher-bearers, we began to sift through the human tragedy, selecting only priority three patients who we knew could be treated quickly at the CCP. We knew that some of the injured left to wait were going to die because of the decisions we made. Jordo had said it was like playing God, deciding who would live and who would be left to die. But to me God no longer existed. All I had was my medical expertise and experience to help me make what I believed were sound judgments about these people. God had nothing to do with it, and if I didn't pick who lived and who died then in all likelihood nobody would survive. That was the only positive I could find in the situation.

Occasionally one of the infantry soldiers asked why they could not take a particular casualty and we had to ask them to trust our judgment. Although there was some grumbling, they accepted it and allowed us to get on with our job. We were feeling bad enough already without others questioning our decisions. From their point of view, it must have been hard to stand by and watch two medics discussing an injured person and then deciding not to treat them before moving on to someone else.

During our first sweep of the area we assessed the situation as a whole to get a better idea of the types of wounds and the number of injured, because we couldn't afford to get stuck in one section if there was another nearby that required more attention. The injuries, caused mainly by gunshots and machetes, were horrific. The smell was reminiscent of a rotting garbage dump on an extremely hot day. All around the MSF ward were injured people lying in blood and human waste. But everything I'd seen during the previous couple of days had begun to make me immune to it all. In my mind, the situation was starting to become normal. The only way I can describe the change in me is that I'd had a kind of "mind shift". The injured and dead had become a series of different injuries to be remembered rather than people. We would walk around and say things like "Take that arm", or "Take the head injury, leave that leg and don't worry about that face". We would tread on something soft, only to find it was a person under the rubbish. Sometimes they were dead, sometimes they were badly wounded. A lot of them were children or babies. The sheer amount of rubbish made it difficult to find, or even recognise, some of the casualties.

We would gather about fifteen people to be stretchered away for treatment by the CCP. When we were sure it was coping, we went back and identified another fifteen to twenty. And then we did it again and again. With the CCP now supported by the extra staff, the number of casualties being treated increased. When it could no longer cope we would stop, have a drink or help out. This went on for the whole day. We followed the same route around the MSF hospital and compound so many times that we had memorised who was where and the wounds they had suffered. As we went back to get more injured we make decisions like, "Remember the girl with bilateral fractured tib and fibs. And the man with the head wound. Well, we'll get them this time." Sometimes we would find that they had died or simply vanished in the meantime.

Brett and I would occasionally try and make a joke of everything. I didn't really understand at the time but my black humour was a reaction to the stress of the situation. As we walked around the ward we kept coming across one particular body of a man. It was an extremely hot day and the body had obviously been there for a while because it was quite bloated and had taken on a bit of a green tinge. Each time we passed, we would each kick his foot and tell him he was a lazy bastard and he had to get up. Next time we passed, it would be, "Still here, you lazy prick?" followed by another nudge to the foot. "Look at him now; he's really green with envy." Eventually the body was taken away by the Zambians and buried in a mass grave. When we passed the empty space, I said, "About time you got up and pissed off".

One casualty had been shot through both buttocks, so Brett decided that he had to go directly to Carol for treatment. We nicknamed him "Arse Bandit". Sometime later back in Kigali, she sarcastically thanked Brett for his thoughtfulness. To somebody who has never been in such a situation our reaction may seem disrespectful and perhaps even bizarre. It was neither of those things. Looking back it was clearly a way of coping mentally with the horror of it all. Being in that situation was absolutely horrendous. Having to make decisions I knew would cost the lives of some of the people I was trying to save, was mind-blowing. I believe you either fall apart or you put all your personal recourses and put your strengths to best use. I believe making light of the horror was something I did because I could not afford to fall apart. I had a job to do. I was a soldier, a sergeant and a senior medic. But most of all I was Australian, and we don't fall apart. I couldn't let my team down and I needed to lead by example. And I didn't know it then, but the experience was damaging me in ways I would only discover years later back home.

One of the choppers that arrived to evacuate casualties brought in our Commanding Officer (CO) and the Regimental Sergeant Major (RSM), accompanied by a small group of journalists, including the BBC and CNN. The journalists got busy filming and getting their story while the CO and RSM had a look around. All they knew was what they had heard over the radios. Now they wanted some first-hand information. The RSM had brought his video camera so I asked if I could show him some things I thought would interest him. I took him to the compound and identified some of the casualties, giving descriptions of their injuries. We had assessed a man with a fractured femur and elbow as a priority one casualty. The RSM filmed as I showed him the extent of the wounds and explained how the man was assessed. We left him there and after showing the RSM a few more casualties we went back to the CCP where I got to work on a woman with a fractured femur. The RSM helped me straighten out her leg. After I applied traction to the fractured leg he held both legs in position until I successfully secured the fractured leg to the good one with a makeshift splint. CNN later offered him $300 for each foot of film he had shot, but he wouldn't have a bar of it. As the CO and RSM were leaving on the next chopper, Jordo and Churchy thought it was an excellent opportunity to send out a few more casualties. They got them down to the landing zone in the ambulance and loaded them onto the chopper, but then had to watch in sheer frustration as the casualties were removed to allow several journalists and their cameras space to get out of the camp. All Jordo and Churchy could do was bring the casualties back to the holding area to wait for a truck that would take them to Butare hospital.

While this was going on, the RPA were quietly retrieving the dead and burying them in mass graves. We believed it was to lower the body count, and they had been at it since the night before. To regain control of their area, the Zambians were doing the same. They collected hundreds of dead just to clear the road so vehicles could access the area. All of these bodies went into mass graves as well. Even our own infantry had to do it. I have no doubt it was the worst thing they have ever done – picking up the putrefying, horrifically damaged bodies of men, women and children and throwing them into a large pit already half full of other dead. It was like something out of a black-and-white Nazi concentration camp film, except it was very real and in vivid, awful colour. The process was filthy, disgusting and degrading to the dead, and would scar many of the soldiers for the rest of their lives.

Later that day I was tasked by the new infantry commander, a captain, to take a truck to the water point area and conduct triage. It wasn't all that far from the house we had first worked out of near the RPA checkpoint. I took three infantry soldiers with me for protection. My orders were to collect no more than fifteen casualties and I had a time limit of thirty minutes to assess, collect, treat and evacuate them. In a way I felt a little honoured that I had been given the responsibility to make all the decisions myself, to use all my training as a soldier and medic. When we arrived at the water point a Zambatt lance corporal directed us down a steep embankment beside the road to show me where to retrieve the casualties. I began my triage, selecting the injured I thought needed to go so the infantry blokes could carry them back up the hill to the truck supplied by the Zambians. I picked my way through the mountains of rubbish and blue plastic tarps that had once been shelters. Sometimes the rubbish would shift beneath me and I would find another casualty for the truck, or another dead body of which there were hundreds. It's hard to describe how I was feeling, but one incident shows how I was thinking. I was so preoccupied with doing negative triage that when I discovered a newborn baby, barely 48 hours old, I believed I had no choice but to leave him behind. I thought back to the young babies Brett and I had abandoned in the MSF ward. Leaving them had been a nightmare, but I believed we were not ultimately responsible for that decision. The doctor had made the decision when we had asked permission to bring the babies out. She was the one who said no. This time it was different. I was the sole person responsible for making a decision about this baby's life. At the time I thought, *"Fuck, here we go again. What the hell am I to do?"* I felt overwhelming guilt about leaving this tiny child behind and the one constructive thing I could think of doing was covering him with something so he would not get sunburnt. Perhaps a little bit of comfort in the whole horrible situation. I grabbed some blue plastic and completely covered the baby while making sure he would not suffocate. I quietly said to him, "Sorry, but you are probably better off dying here peacefully than at the hands of the RPA if you are found." Then I blanked the whole situation from my mind and continued with the work I was supposed to be doing. It's strange how the mind works.

As I headed back up the hill to the truck, an injured man jumped in front of me. He had a severe head wound which had left some of his brain exposed. I was not going to take him because any exposure of the brain made him a priority one, but he was practically begging me. I was helping another casualty and just did not have the energy or strength to help him as well. I told him he could go as long as he made his own way up the steep embankment and onto the back of the truck. Somehow he managed to stagger and weave his way up to the truck where he was helped into the back. He made his way towards the front and quietly sat down on the seat and leaned his injured head against the woodwork. A woman shot through both knees was carefully lifted into the back as well. She did not want to go but we grabbed her. A woman who had been shot through the ankle simply refused to go and hobbled off. The Zambatt lance corporal said an injured father and son were around the corner. When we got there they were nowhere to be seen. The Zambian thought they had probably been buried alive by the RPA, and he pointed to a spot about 50 metres behind the buildings where he said there was a mass grave. At the time I did not think this was strange. Considering what the RPA had already done, I had no doubt he was telling the truth. Later, when I reported this to our infantry captain, he told me it was all bullshit and refused to believe it. He had only arrived that day and was probably not aware of what the RPA where capable of doing. I certainly was and I had no doubt.

Next we moved to a house where I was told an injured mother and baby needed help. When I entered the room I was amazed to find her sitting amongst what appeared to be several hundred infants. She was attempting to breastfeed her own child and many of the others were crawling over her in a pathetic attempt to feed as well. I think they could smell her breast milk. It reminded me of ants crawling all over a carcass. The poor woman was so exhausted that she didn't bother to stop them. I managed to get her up and outside with her child when she suddenly decided to return for something. I was hoping she didn't have more children of her own because the truck was full and I had just reached my half-hour time limit. I needed to get out of there. She returned with a few flimsy belongings in a small shoulder bag.

Back at the CCP, Nico was working on a casualty with an air force nursing officer who had just arrived as part of the second CCP sent in to help. When they decided to put in a drip, she asked him to pass an alcohol swab to sterilise the area. He said: "You're fucking joking! We ran out of them days ago. Just use water and get the thing in." She was stunned and horrified, but I think it gave her some inkling of the situation we had confronted during the past few days.

My time was up so we returned to the CCP where Jordo climbed on the back to assess the casualties I had collected. He told me two of them were dead: the man with the head wound and the woman shot through both knees. I was shattered. Both had appeared well enough when we loaded them. I was also a bit dark on myself, thinking that maybe I had selected the wrong casualties. I knew I shouldn't have taken the man because he was priority one. I felt I had let myself down by not refusing his pleas, but I had to push that out of my mind and get back to my job. I went to the infantry captain to get permission to fetch more casualties from the water point but he said no, so I hooked up with Brett again and we went back to doing triage of the MSF ward and compound area. A woman with horrific facial injuries wanted to use the toilets which had been set up by the NGOs about a hundred metres away in an area surrounded by hessian. She needed a drip and I could not let her go because there were no escorts available. I told her she would just have to wee on the edge of the truck. It was then we learned some of the internally displaced persons (IDPs) had hidden in the toilet trenches to avoid being killed during the shooting the previous day. Jordo and his group had the unenviable task of retrieving them. Neck deep in shit, they had to be roped out and cleaned up. One IDP had apparently hung himself in the toilet area rather than risk being shot. Brett and I checked it out and sure enough he was dead, and had been for a day or so. We got his body down and it was taken away to be buried. It was just another reminder how desperate these poor people must have felt.

I was determined to go back to the water point area. The captain reluctantly gave me permission once I explained I wanted to retrieve some of the children from the building where I had found the injured mother and hand them over to the Red Cross. I was given 10 minutes, a Land Rover and strict instructions: don't bring back any more injured because we would be leaving Kibeho soon and would not have time to treat them. I grabbed three infantry blokes and we returned to get some of the kids out. There were so many and I had so little time I could not decide which ones to take. In the end I just grabbed any baby wearing a shirt. That way I could hold more of them in my hands at the same by gripping them by the scruff of the shirt. I took as many as I could and put them on the ground behind the Red Cross truck so they could be registered and loaded on board. These children were supposed to be sent to orphanages around the country. We certainly hoped so. As with everyone in Kibeho, these children were badly dehydrated. One of the Zambian soldiers opened a water bottle and they all started to crawl towards him as if they could smell the water.

Finally it dawned on me how I had left the newborn baby down the embankment covered in plastic. I was consumed by a desperate need to find him. While my soldiers were helping with the children, I went back down to retrieve the baby. At the bottom I looked up to try and identify the sandbag bunker I had picked a reference point. To my horror there were six bunkers and I could not remember which one I had used. The only thing I could do was walk back and forth, looking under each and every scrap of blue plastic. And there were literally thousands of pieces, the remains of the destroyed shelters.

After a few minutes of searching around, an Australian lance-corporal, who had just arrived in a truck, came down to see what I was doing. When I explained that I was looking for a baby he began to help. Every few metres we stopped to listen and eventually he reckoned he could hear something. We found the baby under the very piece of plastic we were standing on. Christ, I was so happy all I could was blurt out: "You little bloody beauty." I shook his hand so hard I nearly broke his arm off at the elbow. "My hearing has never failed me yet," he said. It had been like looking for the proverbial needle in a haystack except this time we found the needle. With the Land Rover now full, we took seven small children and the baby back to the CCP where they were to be handed to the NGOs. I figured that since they didn't require any treatment it would be all right. To our amazement, not one of the NGOs would take any of them. They refused to acknowledge us when we tapped on their vehicle windows and even wound the windows up to avoid us. We were left with no choice but to put the children on the back of a truck with other casualties, hoping they would survive the long and painful two-hour journey to Butare.

Very late in the afternoon, I spotted an NGO driver who had a vehicle full of blankets. I walked over and asked what he was doing. He told me they were a donation from one of the humanitarian organisations and he just wanted to get rid of them. They were supposed to be for the IDPs, but this was not allowed by the RPA. Instead he was going to dump them right where he stood. I told him to throw them in the back of my Land Rover, because I could get them back to Kigali where our hospital could use them. Back in Kigali I gave the Rwandan part of our hospital 150 new blankets. I kept one. It was cleaned in our laundry facility and I still have it today. The rest I took to Mother Teresa's orphanage.

It was starting to get late so we had to pack up and leave. As the convoy passed through the checkpoints and roadblocks, the RPA checked each vehicle to ensure we only had injured on board. Somehow Jordo managed to smuggle out a small girl by covering her in bandages and putting her on a blanket shelf in the ambulance. Nico tucked away a small child he'd found wandering stark naked down the road. It was a small victory for us. At Zambatt Bravo Company position we set up stretchers and rolled out sleeping bags before trying to relax, eat and drink some brews. The adrenalin rush of yesterday was a distant memory and exhaustion had set in. Even so, sleep that night was hard to come by.

The next morning we prepared to return to Kibeho, but it was not to be. Carol was told we had to remain where we were. The second CCP team would take over our work and they headed off, leaving us behind. We were disappointed and extremely frustrated. We knew that two CCPs working together could achieve so much more. All we could do was sit around the radio and listen to the group in Kibeho and wonder why we weren't there. Carol contacted headquarters and asked for permission for us to return and help but it was refused. They thought that we were over-stressed and deserved a rest. We were ordered to return to Kigali. Before we left, another Australian infantry platoon arrived by road to take over from Lieutenant Tilbrook's group. With them was a new evacuation team with an ambulance full of stores that would take over from Jordo and Churchy. My friend Eric arrived with a section to start tackling the environmental health issues poised to erupt. A couple of cooks arrived with their field kitchen and rations. It looked like the Australians were going to stay and finish the job of getting the Kibeho camp closed. What a pity my team and I would not be there to see it.

An SAS medic and his offsider pulled up in their ambulance. Without thinking I told them when they arrived at Kibeho they should hook in because there were plenty of "Training aids lying all over the place". What I was trying to say was their knowledge of medical procedures was going to be fully stretched, because there were so many different types of casualties who needed treatment. I realised that once again I had dehumanised the IDPs. I had just blurted out another dickhead thing that I regretted immediately. The new convoy departed for Kibeho with extra stores and fresh staff and we sat back again to listen to the radio. When Lieutenant Tilbrook's platoon returned we packed up all our personal gear, did a complete weapons check and boarded our vehicles for the journey back to Kigali headquarters. The Land Rover and trailer I had used for the past week stayed behind with the CSM so I travelled on the back of the truck with one of the infantry sections. I felt proud to sit with the young soldiers. We had all been through something that was very hard to comprehend. It was the last I would see of Kibeho, although during the next four months I would see many of our patients at the Ausmed hospital and many young IDPs at the orphanage.

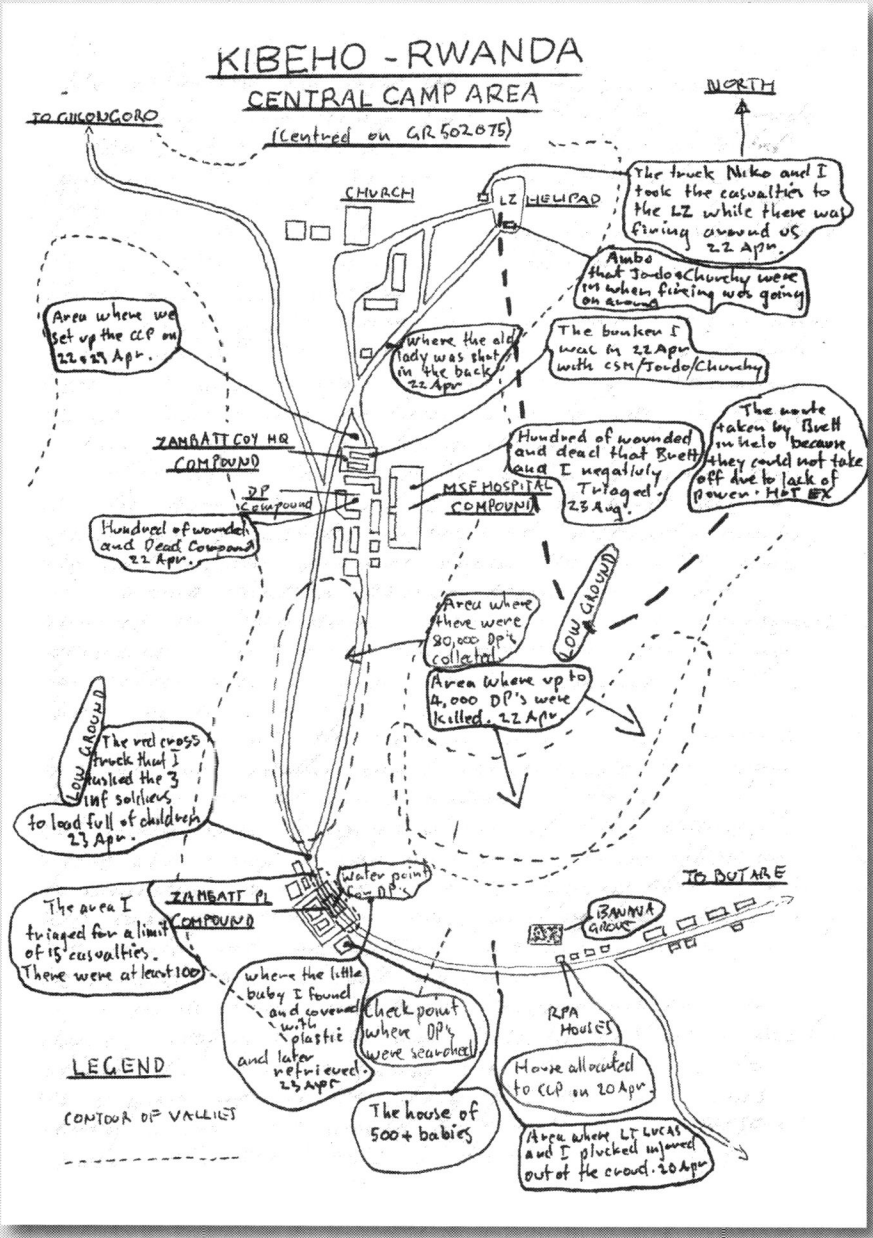

Above. This map from my diary, which I kept each day during my tour of duty in Rwanda, I copied the map from my CSM's note book and then inserted my own information as I remembered it. It shows the triage area and various other places where specific events took place over the four days leading up to, during, and two days after the massacre in Kibeho camp.

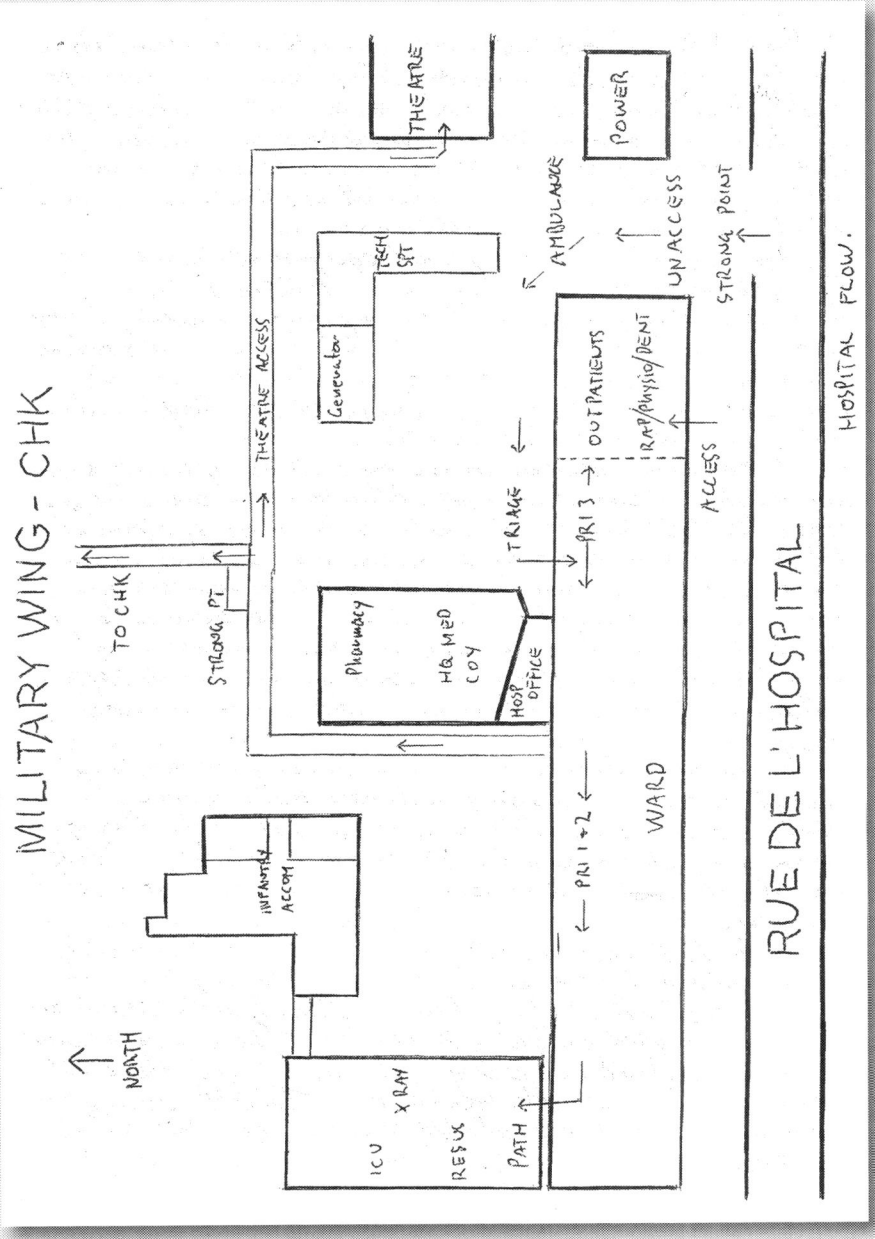

Above. The plan of the Australian hospital setup in part of the Kigali Central Hospital (CHK). Our part was surrounded by razor wire and had strong points at all entry points manned by our soldiers. A platoon of infantry was rotated each week to supply security for the facility and stayed at the hospital.

Above. The night brought welcome rest and a chance for food and coffee for the casualty clearing post team that was present during the Kibeho Massacre. From left Corporal Tim Whyte, Captain Carol Vaughan-Evens, Corporal Milan Nikolic and myself.

Above. One of the hundreds of casualties that were evacuated to the casualty clearing post from the makeshift NGO hospital to be treated. Sergeant Brett Dick and myself in the middle are being escorted by some of the 2RAR soldiers as we weave our way through rain filled ditches and figure-eight razor wire.

Above. A mass grave was dug up just outside the wall of our hospital complex. At night dogs would run off with the bones and it was not uncommon to see a dog chewing on a human femur the next morning. The photo was taken during a drive past from our vehicle.

Above. A sea of humanity. The IDP's of Kibeho camp were herded to the ridge line were they were meant to go through a check point to be cleared for transportation back to their homes. There was an estimated one hundred and twenty thousand people crammed into a couple of square kilometres without food or water for the five days.

Above. Soldiers keep a watchful eye in search of a sniper shooting victims within the camp.

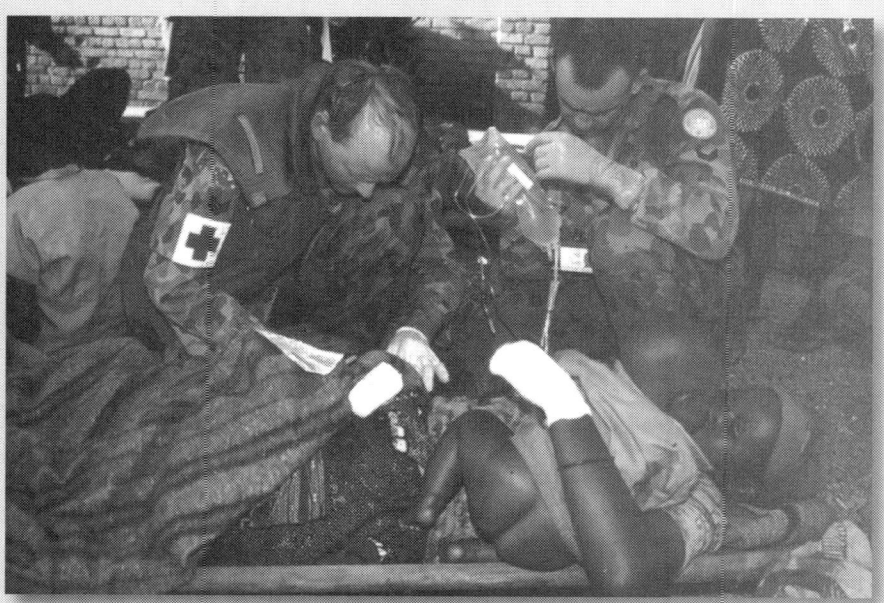

Above. The mother and child were evacuated from the makeshift NGO ward together by stretcher. The mother had been struck on both hands by a machete as she tried to protect her own head as well as her baby. One of the infantry corporals sets up a drip as I start to insert a cannula in a vein in her arm after we had treated her wounds. She was later evacuated by helicopter to Butare hospital, and was one of the last casualties able to be flown out before the massacre started.

Above. As many priority one casualties as possible were evacuated by helicopter with each of us taking turns as escort on board. Others were sent by truck. During periods of intense firing the helicopters were unable to land so we had to hold onto the casualties until firing eased.

Above. The first CCP team continued to work even in the pouring rain. There was no time to stop due to the huge number of casualties that kept being brought to us. We were running out of medical stores and when we ran out of water for cleaning we used buckets of rainwater.

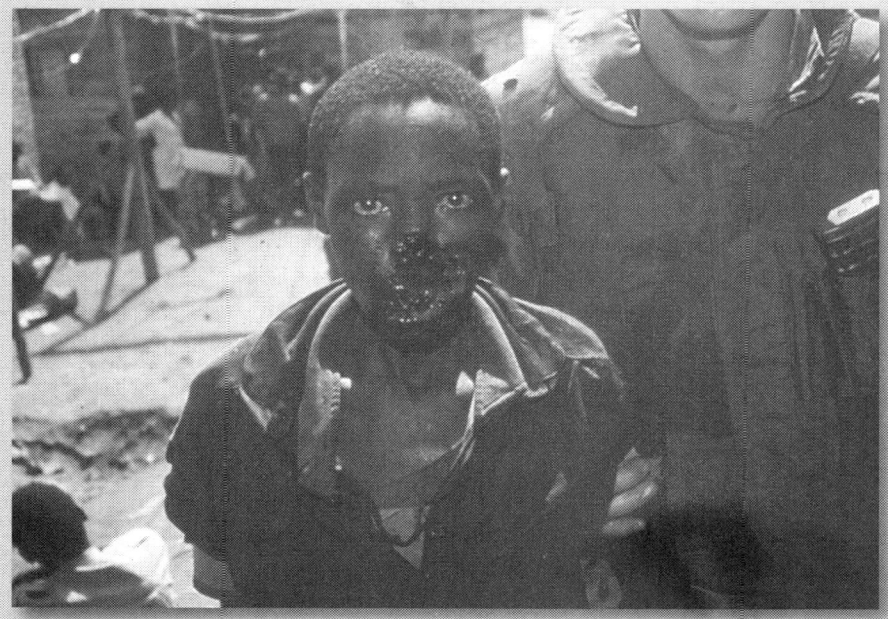

Above. IDP Casualties encountered in the first 24 hours of the massacre.

Above. The sad sight of women and children lying dead was all around the camp.

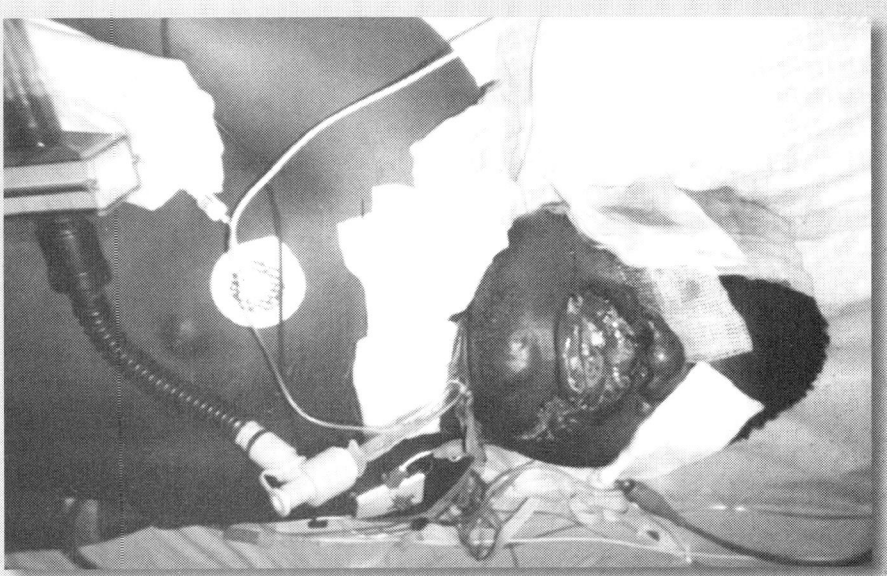

Above. Resus number 112 went through the front windscreen of the car he was travelling in. He suffered major facial injuries and was taken to CHK where he was found by one of our doctors. He had no airway and was not expected to live but through the efforts of our hospital he made a full recovery.

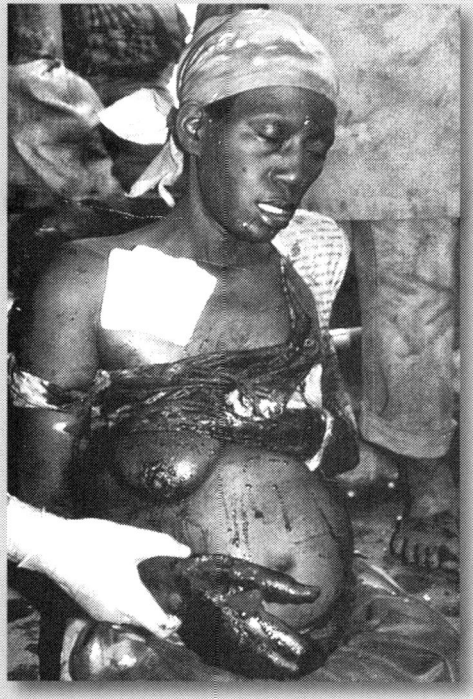

Left. One of the hundreds of seriously wounded casualties from Kibeho. This lady is about twenty-five years old and eight months pregnant. Because she could not move fast enough she was attacked and struck several times with a machete. Her right hand has been severed so badly that her thumb hangs by a thread. She has also been hit in the right shoulder and left upper arm. She was badly dehydrated and semi-conscious before Jordo found her and brought her to the CCP for treatment. She was evacuated by truck to Butare hospital which was a two hour bumpy journey along a dirt road. It is not known whether she survived, as was the case with most of the casualties that were treated.

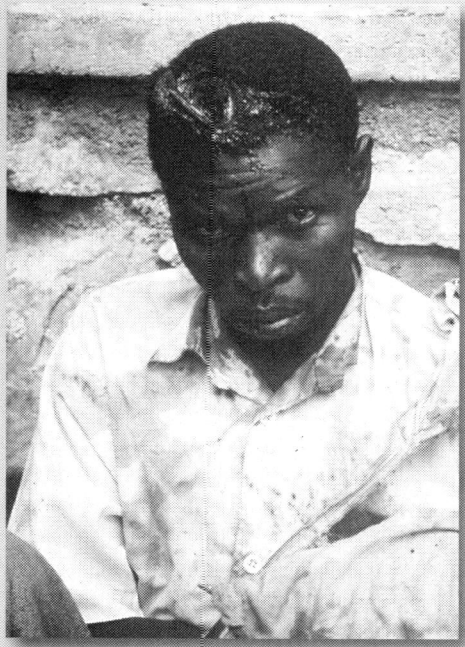

Left. Machete wounds were one of the most common injuries to be treated. This poor man sat waiting to be treated with an open wound to the skull inflicted by a blow to the head with a machete.

Above. One of the many mass graves that had to be dug so that the sheer number of dead could be buried in the hope that any disease would not spread among the living. The dead bodies ranged from babies, children, old men and even pregnant women.

Chapter Seven

Live or die

> *"I often wonder if I chose the 'right' casualties and whether they would all have survived if I'd picked a different two. What happened to the ones left behind? Did I make the right decisions? Could I have made better decisions? It's something you can't afford to dwell on. Letting yourself feel responsible for their deaths only overwhelms you with guilt."*

I watched the countryside pass by as we headed back to Kigali. It was good to be sitting on the back of the vehicle with the infantry blokes instead of driving. It gave me time to think about what had happened and try to make a little sense of it all. It was important to me to recognise that away from the site of the massacre everything else appeared relatively normal. People waved to us from the roadside as we drove past. The kids still yelled out excitedly. It helped me believe that perhaps the Kibeho tragedy was an isolated moment and that hope still existed in this country which had seen so much death. As we rumbled along I reflected on the work we had done and the choices I had to make doing negative triage. So many questions arise when you have the responsibility to decide what priority should be given to casualties depending on the severity of their injuries. Was he a priority one (traumatic amputations, open fractures with profuse bleeding, severe head injuries) likely to die within the hour if he was not evacuated by the fastest possible means for lifesaving surgery? Was she a priority two – not in immediate danger of dying but needing some form of surgery? Was that child a priority three who needs hospitalising for injuries that are not yet life-threatening?

Normal triage involves treating and evacuating casualties so that priority ones, the worst injured, go first followed by priority twos, then threes and then anyone else. In negative triage the senior medical person present deems the area a "mass casualty" situation based on the type and volume of injuries and the medical personnel and equipment available. At Kibeho, Captain Carol Vaughan-Evans had made the decision quickly and confidently. Because of the sheer number of casualties, it had been necessary to evacuate the priority threes first, then priority twos and hopefully the priority ones. It was the only way our team was able to treat the maximum number of casualties with the resources we had and in the quickest possible time.

The task of allocating the priorities was given to me, Sergeant Brett Dick and Jordo. I estimated we each did about 20 "rounds" that day. Of course, you won't get it right every time, but I was still feeling the shock that hit me when Jordo told me two of the injured I'd selected were dead. I often wonder if I chose the "right" casualties and whether they would all have survived if I'd picked a different two. What happened to the ones left behind? Did I make the right decisions? Could I have made better decisions? It's something you can't afford to dwell on. Letting yourself feel responsible for their deaths only overwhelms you with guilt. Still, they were questions I found difficult to answer as we headed further and further away from Kibeho.

I had been trained to make fast decisions. Despite the indescribable conditions you have to try not to let emotion intrude while all the while guarding against losing your compassion. That was why I had to say no to the woman who kept asking us to take her injured daughter. But I also told the mother that next time we might be able to take her daughter, and I hoped at the time it was the truth. I found I had to be firm with my fellow soldiers while taking the time to explain why one casualty could be stretchered away and why another could not. I found out how very important it was to discuss each case quickly when working with other medical personnel before moving on. Speed is vital when trying to save so many lives but the huge responsibility and standards required for effective triage must never be forgotten. I was thankful for all the medical training I had received and the experiences I'd been through before Rwanda which went some way towards preparing me. Under such severe stress and the constant threat of gunfire, mistakes were made but we just had to carry on. You can never give in to despair. You can rest, or even fall apart, after the job is done. I had seen first-hand how to use every resource available – manpower, vehicles, stores and knowledge – to get the best possible outcome. It had reinforced to me the value of people who take control and act decisively to make sure the people working under them achieve the results they need. You must learn from errors of judgment and stay focused on the job. There is no point arguing if someone is not in the position to help with transport. Instead you must quickly search for some other means. It may, as it was in my case, be necessary to simply order a driver with a truck to do something. It can be frustrating and infuriating, but in the middle of such carnage is not the place to show emotion. The most important thing was finding a means of evacuation so lives could be saved. In my opinion making such choices made a difference when it came to saving lives at Kibeho, a place where the death toll will never be accurately known.

At Kibeho the medical team treated hundreds and hundreds of casualties. The perpetrators did not discriminate. We helped babies, children, pregnant women, adults and the elderly. Their injuries were caused by machetes, guns, mortars, RPGs, knives, shrapnel and much more. Some wounds were simple, some complicated. Most casualties had a combination. Each and every victim was undernourished and dehydrated. The RPA had cut off the water supply four days before we arrived in the camp. Food was so scarce that people were reduced to picking through human faeces for pieces of undigested food. Some women re-cooked it for children. Some kids just ate what they found then and there. It was a truly miserable sight.

The medical personnel worked equally well as a team or on their own, even when the CCP was overwhelmed. I will never forget Corporal Tim Whyte treating 24 casualties by himself in one day, including three at the same time against the brick wall of a building we were using as protection from the shooting going on all around us. Corporal Milan Nikolic looked after 27 wounded in the back of a truck, checking on bandages and changing drips, whilst also trying to document the casualties. I don't know how many I treated. We tried to maintain records as much as possible but as the casualty count mounted we just didn't have the time.

In my personal journal I kept while in Rwanda, I made a note of the ones that struck a chord with me and how I dealt with them:

"…a female about 40 years old with a severe machete wound to face. She had been struck so hard with a machete just on the bridge of her nose that it had fractured her top jaw which now lay forward of the rest of her face, completely exposing her airway. As she tried to speak you could see her tongue moving through the hole in her face. She wasn't complaining of any pain and there was very little bleeding, suggesting that the wound was a day or two old. All she wanted was a drink of water and to go to the toilet. I put up a drip and she went to the toilet on the edge of the truck. I decided it was unsafe for her to go to the latrines due to the amount of gunfire still going on in the compound, and also the difficulty of getting her escorted there and back. No bandages could be applied due to the danger of completely cutting off her airway. She was evacuated to Butare with seven other priority one casualties on one of the evac choppers with me and Nico doing the escort…

"…a male about 11 years old with a sucking chest wound. Jordo had rescued the boy and placed him on the truck that Nico was in while there was gunfire all around. I looked up while I was treating someone else when the boy fell off the truck and Nico said from in the back of the truck, 'Leave him. He's dead'. Jordo could not believe it so I went over and the boy moved so Jordo and I got stuck in. The first thing Jordo did was put in a false airway and then we started to seal the chest wound, using a huge roller bandage and put a drip up. Carol took over from me as Jordo administered morphine. The boy became semi-conscious and had a lot difficulty in breathing. He was evacuated with others by chopper to Kigali, and operated on that day to remove shrapnel from chest. One piece of shrapnel could not be removed. He spent a week in ICU and then transferred to the ward. After another week he developed pneumonia, spent a further week in ICU before finally being discharged and transferred to Mother Teresa's orphanage…

"...a 30-year-old male. He had been extracted from the ward during breaks in the firing and on examination I found he had a fractured left humerus complicated with arterial bleeding. I applied indirect pressure to the brachial artery which stopped the bleeding effectively and then direct pressure was applied using a shell dressing covered with a roller bandage. I put a drip up and elevated the arm before strapping it to his body. The doctor wanted to check the wound so I applied indirect pressure again and took down the dressing. She checked the wound and once again I dressed it. He was then evacuated by chopper with other patients to Butare ...

"...a woman over 50 years old, suffering a closed fractured left femur. She was removed from the ward during the period that Brett and I were conducting negative triage. On examination I found there was six inches of shortening of the left leg. I applied traction and brought the leg into line with the other leg and then got the RSM to hold the leg. I applied a figure-eight bandage to secure the ankles together then using an improvised splint made from a log, roller bandaged the whole leg to it. She was stable but dehydrated so I put a drip up. I didn't administer any morphine because she was in very little pain. She was placed on a stretcher and moved by truck to Butare which was a two hour drive away...

"...a man approximately 40 years old...on examination I found he had about 12 inches of intestine protruding from a laceration in his abdomen caused by a blow from a machete. He was not in any other distress. I treated him by applying a ring bandage around the exposed intestines and then covering the whole lot up with a light moist dressing. I put a drip up and administered morphine intravenously via the drip. He was evacuated to Butare by truck in a sitting position on a stretcher...

"...a 30-year-old male suffering from gunshot wounds to the right upper leg and left arm...we came across this man and decided to leave him because he was priority one. At the time he was semi-conscious and had a strong pulse but he had lost a hell of a lot of blood. Later that day he was collected by one of the stretcher teams and brought to the CCP. On examination he was found to have a completely shattered left elbow caused by gunshot and his right femur was badly fractured – also caused by gunshot. By the look of the wounds he had been shot at very close range. Direct pressure was applied using roller bandages to all wounds and a drip was put up. Morphine was administered intravenously by the drip and he was eventually evacuated by truck to Butare...

"…a small boy aged about seven who had been shot in the chest – one of the most amazing survivors of the massacre I had seen. This boy had walked up from the ward and tapped me on the arm. I was a little amused at first to see him grabbing at my shirtsleeve and wondered what he wanted. Then, when he turned sideways and pointed at the left-hand side of his chest, I understood clearly what he wanted. There was a medium-sized entry wound in the front left of his chest and when I turned him around I saw he had a very large exploded exit wound in the back left of his rib cage. All his shattered ribs were well exposed and I could clearly see his damaged lung. Strangely enough he did not seem distressed at all. He just wanted me to fix him. I stood for a moment absolutely stunned and wondered how the hell this boy was still alive with half his chest missing, let alone being able to walk around. All I could think of doing was wrapping his upper body up in roller bandages to try and keep everything reasonably in place. I tried to get a drip in but due to dehydration from the amount of blood he had lost he had venous shutdown and I could not get a vein anywhere. He was evacuated to Butare on the next available chopper…

"…an 11-year-old girl was being carried by her mother on her back, piggyback style. The mother just wanted her to be seen and treated by us but because she was priority two we left her many times until the end of the day. The girl had suffered severe machete wounds to both her legs. She had been struck repeatedly and the tibia and fibula in both legs were fractured. I could clearly see the smashed bones. I carried her out in my arms just as the RPA moved in. I had to tell her mother that she had to stay behind. I was exhausted by the time I had weaved my way in and out of razor wire fences and got her to the CCP for treatment….I dressed both legs and then splinted them together. I put up a drip and since she didn't seem distressed I didn't give her any morphine. She was eventually evacuated by truck to Butare…

"…a woman about 30 years old was found by Churchy and me in the MSF ward. She had huge lacerations on her upper and lower left arm that she had used to fend off machete blows directed at her head. She had some major arterial bleeding….We applied several shell dressings for direct pressure to stem the flow of blood and then put up a drip. On examination we couldn't detect any fractures and she was eventually evacuated to Butare by truck…

"…a man approximately 30 years of age had severe lacerations to both lower arms and hands. He suffered these as he tried to protect himself from machete hits to the face. The lacerations went through the palms of both his hands and severed some of the tendons, which were clearly visible. Both his arms and hands were fully bandaged with roller bandages to apply direct pressure and he was also evacuated by vehicle to Butare...

"...a woman aged about 20 was pregnant and in labour. I found her in the ward and was directed to help her with the birth if necessary. During a break in the gunfire I went down to check on her. She had been having contractions about eight minutes apart but they had now ceased. I just gave her plenty of reassurance and managed to help her out of the ward, placing her on the next available truck for evacuation to Butare...

"...one man about 20 I found sitting in the compound with a laceration to the back of his neck. He was in no distress and just sat quietly. When I checked him I found that his cervical spine was completely exposed and I could see the individual vertebrae. Someone had tried unsuccessfully to chop his head off with a blunt machete. He showed no signs of any neurological problems. All I could do was bandage his neck, passing the roller bandages under his arms so as not to block his airway, and then have him escorted by one of the soldiers up to the truck so he could be evacuated to Butare...

"...a man of 40 years of age suffering bilateral sucking chest wounds. This man was placed in the back of the ambulance with Churchy and Carol. He had bilateral chest injuries caused by gunshot, extreme difficulty in breathing and was losing blood quickly. Churchy put a drip in the left arm but the fluid simply ran out an exposed vein in the neck. He then placed a drip in the right arm. They were unable to dress wounds due to the possibility of restricting the breathing further. Each time the lungs filled up with blood, Churchy would raise the legs and the Carol would compress the chest area to force the blood out of the lungs. This temporarily eased the breathing but didn't last long. This had to be done numerous times during the two-hour drive to Butare before they were finally able to hand him over to local hospital staff...

"...this was the last person I got out of the ward before the RPA banned us from going in, then opened fire. He was a 60-year-old man and had suffered a gunshot wound to the right ankle. I found him in the compound next to the MSF ward where he was hopping around using a stick to help support himself. I helped him by alternating between carrying him and supporting him using myself as a human crutch. We would move 20 metres until he could go no further. I then swapped sides and ended up carrying him. Having to weave in and out of the razor wire I became too exhausted to go and we both fell to the ground just when two infantry soldiers came and took him from me. They carried him the rest of the way to the CCP while I picked myself up and staggered on. I applied shell dressing to his ankle and put a drip up, before he was evacuated...

"...Each time Brett and I searched the MSF hospital we would come across patients that seemed to appear from nowhere. We entered a room that must have been allocated as a women's ward. In one corner were six newborn babies. They could not have been more than 48 hours old. After much discussion we decided to see the boss to ask if we could take them. They were not injured in any way, so really we weren't supposed to take them. We decided to leave them where they were but still ask the boss for her decision because we did not want this on our conscience. On the floor opposite the babies we came across a mother and her small baby. The baby was less than 24 hours old. We told the mother she must leave with the baby because the RPA would be in soon to clear the ward. But she was too stuffed to move. Brett and I left the ward and after finishing this round went and saw the boss about retrieving the babies, and the answer we got was to leave them all. We were not visibly upset but like Brett it played on my mind. We had to continue triaging the whole complex and each time we went into that room we could hear the babies crying. It was a terrible feeling knowing that we could do nothing for them. We'd do a really quick check of the room and piss off as quick as possible. One time we entered and noticed the mother had vanished so we picked up the newborn baby she had left behind and placed it with the other babies. Again we left quickly, not wanting to stay and hear them crying. This went on several times during the day. Walking in and out of that room became torture. Again we explained the situation to the boss and again the answer was no. After a while we decided that there was no way we would go in that room. We'd had enough. Both of us have children and it was getting really upsetting. We understood the boss's decision because we had no means of evacuating them, and we were only treating injured people. Even though neither of us wanted to enter that room again we had to. Later in the day I was sent on another task. When I returned Brett grabbed me and gave me some excellent news. While I was gone two Red Cross trucks turned up with some NGO workers. So he had taken it upon himself, after a quick discussion with the NGOs, to go in and retrieve the babies. He got them all out. Boy, was he happy and I was glad..."

These stories are just the very tip of the iceberg. There were too many horrifically injured to count. We found ourselves trying to treat wounds that in Australia only specialists would see and deal with. And we had no choice but to work as fast as we could with extremely limited resources. When we started running out of supplies and the helicopters could not get in because of the shooting we had no choice but to resort to retrieving bandages from dead people to use on live ones, re-using gloves and washing our hands in rainwater.

This period of April 18—22 April, 1995 was the most testing time of my life both physically and mentally. I believe I did okay. We saved who we could and did our best in the most atrocious conditions. I will never understand Australia's system of honours and awards. There seems to be no explanation why nothing was done for Jordo even though his heroic act of saving that boy from the direct line of fire was recorded. I nominated both Nico and Tim for the Nursing Services Cross, a medal awarded for outstanding medical work. Neither received anything. Instead it was awarded to a sister who worked in the theatre in Kigali. I believe the 32 Australian soldiers present at Kibeho from April 18–22 should be nominated for a group bravery award. I know it can be done retrospectively. I believe it was done for the helicopter crews who saved lives during the tragic Sydney to Hobart yacht race. Of course, that was aired on national television as it happened. We were not seen and we were advised not to talk to the media at all. Perhaps now that the full extent of our mission is out in the open, something will happen one day.

I watched the countryside slip by as we drove back to Kigali. Its stark beauty looked peaceful, a complete contrast to the past week. I almost fell asleep.

Chapter Eight

Finish the job

"He had no answers as to why we could not intervene during the massacre and protect the IDPs with our weapons except that it was a decision from UN headquarters. He did tell us that there was absolutely no doubt if we had not been at Kibeho the whole camp of around 100,000 people probably would have been slaughtered and the world would have been none the wiser."

Our convoy of vehicles carrying some very exhausted soldiers finally arrived at the safety of the Australian headquarters compound in Kigali. Things were looking up before we even dismounted. Major McCrohan walked up to the passenger side of the vehicle I was travelling in and congratulated Lieutenant Tilbrook on a job well done. In the background I heard one of the soldiers ask under his breath what Lieutenant Tilbrook had done that they had not done themselves. I remember thinking that this young lieutenant had just completed the extraordinary job of keeping everyone alive. That unfortunate young soldier seemed not to be aware of all the responsibilities of leadership and the decision-making that went with it. One wrong decision could easily have cost 32 Australian soldiers their lives.

After dismounting and making our way back to our own lines I realised I had left my large pack with all my personal gear, including my sleeping bag, in the Land Rover back in Kibeho. I had to borrow a razor and soap from one of the other sergeants. I showered before weighing myself as I did every week and discovered I had lost seven kilograms during my time at Kibeho. I donned some civilian clothes, handed my weapon and ammunition into the guardroom and headed to the sergeant's mess. All I wanted to do was have a few beers. The CO and the RSM decided to open all the messes so the soldiers who had just returned from Kibeho could enjoy a few quiet ones, even though it was the one alcohol-free day of the week when the messes were normally closed. I bought my first beer and sat down feeling exhausted. A good friend of mine, a female sergeant and Intelligence Corps interpreter, asked me how I was. I started to talk a little about what had happened at Kibeho. She told me that a shot had been fired just outside the front gate of the compound and a man had been killed. I thought, *Shit, a million shots were fired at Kibeho. What was the comparison there? How come they were all uptight about a single shot?* A couple of other sergeants came over to listen but I found it extremely hard to talk about anything. I mentioned a couple of things before it dawned on me that these people had not been there and might not believe some of the things I had to say. Instead I kept quiet. I drank a couple of beers and then went to my room to try and get some sleep. Someone gave me a couple of blankets because I had lost my sleeping bag. I tried to sleep but it would not come. I was still on an adrenalin high. My brain would not shut up. I spent most of the night walking the balcony and drinking my favourite orange tea. Luckily for me, we had set up a brew point so I was able to drink tea all night. Everything was so quiet and still but my mind would not co-operate. I just could not stop thinking about what had happened.

The next morning was Anzac Day and we were all on parade for the early morning dawn service. One of the Indian pipers played the "Last Post". When the wreath-laying ceremony began I felt absolutely stunned and shattered. An RPA captain had been invited to lay a wreath. I was fuming. I could not believe it was happening after the events at Kibeho. The RPA had just murdered about 8,000 helpless men, women and children in cold blood and here was one of their captains laying a wreath as if nothing had happened. I wanted to go down in front of everyone and punch him as hard as I could. Only with a huge amount of effort did I stop myself from moving. I just kept my mouth shut and tried to accept what was a political situation. Later when the service was finished I spoke to some of the soldiers who were with me in Kibeho and they told me they felt exactly the same way.

We all had to work until lunch-time when the Anzac Day celebrations would get underway in the messes with the traditional two up, crown and anchor and other games. I went over to the hospital to work in the CCP but could not focus. All the members of the CCP team were drawn together by the need to talk about Kibeho. For a couple of hours we sat in a small group, drinking coffee and chatting. Unfortunately some of the other people there saw things differently. We heard the odd smartarse comment like, "There are the war heroes" and "Come back to do some real work?" We were all well aware that the hospital had changed to 12-hour shifts to handle the patient load from Kibeho, and that everyone had to work extra-long hours, but there was no need for comments like that.

About mid-morning my company commander called all CCP members to a meeting for a critical debrief on Kibeho. We all sat in a circle while he asked us what we felt and encouraged us to talk about our experiences. Each of us spoke about what we had seen and experienced. As we went on I noticed that the company commander was becoming quite pale and ill. After an hour he was visibly shaken by what we had told him. I think some of us decided at that point not to say a lot more. I asked Carol why Jordo and Churchy were not there. She told me she didn't know but would rectify that straight away.

At midday I went back to my room and got changed into civilian clothing to await the open ng of the messes. I also felt ready to call Tara to see how things were. Our newborn baby daughter, Kelsey, was fine and they were back home with Alanna. I assured Tara I was fine and she told me we had made the headlines back home in reports in the Brisbane *Courier Mail* newspaper about Kibeho. Some of the stories were not quite right but

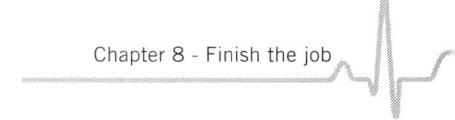

most were fairly accurate. She sent them over to me during the next couple of weeks. A lot of people back home were worried but there was nothing I could do to put their minds at ease.

I felt very alone in my room so I grabbed a couple of diving magazines that had been sent to me and headed over to the kitchen. Sergeant Peter Whitten had been my diving buddy when we had served together in 2nd/14th LHR. I thought some time sitting with him and talking about diving would get my mind off what was troubling me. We had done our diving course together and then spent a couple of weeks in the waters off Tangalooma. He was busy getting a spit-roast ready for the officer's mess when I arrived so I just sat on the steps and chatted to him as he prepared the food. When he started to baste the leg of pork it triggered an instant flashback to a Kibeho casualty I had seen – an above-knee traumatic amputation of the leg. I was about to tell him this but thought better of it. I just left him the magazines and went upstairs to wait for the mess to open. While we were celebrating Anzac Day that evening we all stopped to watch the TV news when a report on the Kibeho massacre suddenly appeared. I watched pictures of our CCP treating casualties, pictures of myself carrying stretchers and visions of the horror of the whole thing. The CNN reporter estimated that as many as 25,000 people had been killed on April 22 and that all the UN had done was stand by and watch. This was pretty distressing and I returned to my room early. I came across Lieutenant Tilbrook who had some cigarettes and asked if I could have one. He gave me a whole packet and I started smoking again. I had not smoked for years but I reckoned I had earned the right to have one.

We had another critical debrief the next morning and this time the company commander was joined by Major Brandy, the medical company second-in-charge. Jordo and Churchy were there. We talked about a few things but not in much emotional depth. I doubt the commander or Major Brandy would have really understood anyway. We were there for about an hour before going back to work. Again, none of us could focus and again we formed a small group, drank brews and talked amongst ourselves about Kibeho. No more RPA shooting had been reported since we left and apparently there were only a couple of hundred IDPs left in the compound. That evening Ausmed Commander Colonel Peter Walfe joined us for a debrief and talked to some of us and the infantry soldiers about what had happened. He had no answers as to why we could not intervene during the massacre and protect the IDPs with our weapons except that it was a decision from UN headquarters. He did tell us that there was absolutely no doubt if we had not been at Kibeho the whole camp of around 100,000 people probably would have been slaughtered and the world would have been none the wiser. He estimated that apart from our lifesaving work, our mere presence in the area had saved more than 65,000 lives. It helped put a more positive perspective on what was disturbing us but for me it still only helped a little. After about 10 days of this most of us started to get back to what we felt was normal. I figured it was time to stop sitting around and just get on with it. Gradually many of us managed to work a full day again.

A couple of soldiers asked if they could exchange their uniforms because they could still smell Kibeho in them no matter how many times they were washed. This was not a problem for the Q-Store but when Nico asked if he could exchange his boots the quartermaster refused and said there was nothing wrong with them. Nico could not stand the thought of wearing them again after treading on so many dead people at Kibeho. I could not see the problem with exchanging the boots if it made Nico happy. I quietly visited a friend who happened to be a sergeant at the Q-Store and explained it to him. He said if that was all Nico wanted after all the shit he had been through then he would gladly help. Nico got his new boots. Some of the soldiers also got new sleeping bags.

A lot of very important people visited Kibeho camp to see for themselves what was going on there. The UN force commander visited early on along with a number of political figures. One day I was surprised to discover our Land Commander of Australia, Major General Peter Arnison, and the RSM of the Army were visiting. I ran into the RSM in the sergeant's mess and had a nice chat with him over a couple of quiet beers. It was good to know that Australia was looking out for its own and their visit was greatly appreciated by all the soldiers. The Australian contingent was highly praised in many different places for how well we had performed in Kibeho. Letters started to arrive on the CO's desk which he forwarded to the companies for all the soldiers to read. In medical company we pinned some of the letters on our notice board. There were letters from commanders at all levels, including the force commander himself. They all said well done to everyone present from April 18—22. One of the nursing officers from the second CCP that replaced my group was disappointed it did not include the time she was there.

During the next couple of weeks more than a hundred of our soldiers rotated through the Kibeho camp. When each group returned to Kigali I asked them for updates about what was happening there. It turned out that an Australian field kitchen had been set up to provide the soldiers with fresh meals every day and they were allowed to go to the Zambian messes for beers on returning from Kibeho each night. There was no more shooting. The camp was eventually closed after four weeks. Everyone returned to Kigali and I even got my personal pack back.

While on duty at the hospital one night I was sitting on the balcony quietly talking to the CSM when he told me how he had stood between an RPA soldier and the person the soldier had just shot. The CSM had told the soldier to go away and leave him to look after the casualty. I was a little bemused by him telling me this but did not say anything. I thought, *So what? Didn't the CSM know many people had done something similar?* Jordo had plucked a child out of the line of fire. Tim had worked on several casualties at once while the wall he was against was peppered with bullets. Nico looked after numerous casualties on the back of a truck and kept working during the fire fight. Carol repeatedly ventured into the MSF hospital to retrieve casualties even though she was ordered by the RPA to stop or she would be killed. Several soldiers were fired on by a sniper. One soldier grabbed a stick an RPA soldier was using to beat an IDP, snapped it in half and told the soldier to "Fuck off". I had treated many casualties while intense firing went on all around us and had sat in front of casualties to protect them from incoming fire while waiting at the landing zone for the next chopper. I had even escorted truckloads of casualties to the LZ on foot amid the shooting. Lieutenant Tilbrook frequently stood between the RPA and the casualties. Everyone had tried to do something.

On May 2, I was in the ward when all the infantry soldiers suddenly started running in different directions. I stopped one and asked what was going on. He told me everyone had been told to "stand to" which meant our unit was on extremely high alert. All the infantry soldiers went to their designated defensive positions and the ward staff followed procedure by herding patients into rooms that did not have windows. We were told there was going to be a demonstration by local people outside the Australian headquarters compound and a march past the hospital compound in protest at the Australian soldiers having stood by and watched the Kibeho tragedy unfold. I went to the roof and watched the march. There was a lot of loud chanting but it was peaceful. After the threat had passed the unit was stood down.

Just before going on stand down on May 3, the commanding officer asked everyone who had been in Kibeho during the massacre to write a statement. He said he wanted them by that evening. I did not know where to start so I just began writing down everything I could remember on a piece of paper. It took me a couple of hours to get it all into a decent statement but there was so much I missed. It felt like the days had become muddled in my mind and I struggled to remember half of what had happened. I felt pressured to complete the statement as fast as possible and hand it in. I forgot to even mention what Jordo had done. I managed six pages. Others only wrote half a page, while Corporal Tiddy almost wrote a book. I did not know at the time the statements would be used by the Defence Force for the nomination of honours and awards otherwise I would have taken a lot more time and care.

The Defence Force sent over a four-person psych team to help debrief the soldiers who had been in Kibeho. Each soldier was interviewed. The team held debriefs on both a group and an individual basis and we filled out numerous surveys designed to find out how we were coping. I took the opportunity to talk to the psychologist several times to get a few things off my chest but it did not seem to help much. I still felt pretty fragile at times and found it hard to work. I had also started having nightmares. While Nico and I made plans for a 72-hour stand down in Nairobi, Kenya, we began working again at the orphanage. My driver's licence meant we could now go whenever we pleased. The first time we drove there several loud explosions went off on the hill next to the road. We nearly jumped out of the vehicle to take cover before realising it was just old ammunition set off by a small grass fire. Shaken, we laughed off our nervousness and continued on our way to the orphanage.

Nico and I finally headed off to Nairobi where we were going to share a room with big Corporal Chris Stindle. We boarded the C130 Hercules aircraft, and after a crude safety brief by the Russian aircrew, flew to Nairobi airport where we were met by the Australian liaison officer who got us settled in our hotel. This officer also booked us in for safaris and other tourist trips when all we wanted to do was get drunk. It was the first time we felt completely safe. We could let our hair down and try to get some good rest. I spent the first day in the hotel bar drinking copious amounts of beer. I was trying hard to wipe out my memories of Kibeho, but with little success. Despite a massive hangover the next day I managed to go on the safari. Nico missed out because I couldn't wake him up. Nico was so sick from our drinking session the night before that he spent most of the morning recovering in bed. The safari was one of the most amazing things I have ever done. I got to see hippos and lions, and even drove slowly through a herd of giraffes. At the end I touched a baby hippo at the zoo and watched lions playing with car tyres as if they were small toys. When the liaison officer phoned and asked why Nico had not made it I said he had food poisoning. When he asked if I was sure it was not caused by too much beer I naturally reminded him I was a sergeant medic. I said I knew what food poisoning was, and anyway would I lie to him about something so serious? Of course not!

The next day I ran into Tim Whyte, who was on stand down at a different hotel. He told me gunshots had been fired in the shopping mall when someone had tried to rob the jewellers and he had just run as fast as he could to get out of there. Nico and I returned to the bar for our next beer-drinking session and bumped into the air force nursing officer from the second CCP that replaced us in Kibeho. After a few beers Nico began giving her a hard time and getting stuck into her about the time she had asked for alcohol swabs. I got him out of that bar and into another to settle him down. We spent the last day touring Nairobi before boarding the Hercules back to Kigali. I had spent the bulk of three days drinking and sleeping but it had done nothing to burn the images of Kibeho out of my mind. I was due to go back to Brisbane on leave in a week to see my new baby and my family. I was worried about how I was going to handle my own newborn after seeing the devastation of children and babies in Kibeho. Would she remind me of the dead and injured babies I had seen? Would I love her? Would I even be able to handle her? I was scared to go home but I knew it was something I had to face. I talked to the psych team and our Padre about these feelings but no one was able to give me a satisfactory answer. In fact, the Padre broke down and cried when I told him some of the things I had seen and experienced. Basically, I was told I would just have to hope for the best. Leave came and went very quickly. Tara had been in hospital and was only discharged the day I arrived. All my fears subsided when I saw Kelsey for the first time. She was beautiful. I applied for a week of emergency leave through Army Community Services and was able to spend it at home before heading back. It was a wonderful time but I felt I had to get back and finish what had been started. I did not want to let my team members down by not returning. Back in Kigali I received a warm welcome. Some people told me they thought I was not coming back and they would have understood if I had not. I just wanted to get on with my job and finish the tour. My company commander asked me to keep an eye on the team that had been in Kibeho and asked me to find out if we all wanted to go to Nairobi as a group. I spoke to each person but the consensus was no because nobody wanted to be singled out. We had been shown a lot of respect by other members of the unit and all of us wanted to just keep working.

Sadly at this time two of my mates were battling. While I was away, Nico had been involved in a terrible vehicle accident. After emergency surgery in Kigali, he was repatriated back to Australia to recover. Meanwhile, my friend Eric was hit by personal tragedy. He was rushed home when one of his young children died in a swimming pool accident. He wanted to come back to Rwanda but the Army said no and replaced him with another health inspector. Several other soldiers did not return from leave for various reasons. Some came back as single men because their relationships had broken up.

At the 12-week mark of the tour it was time to change the teams around. The company commander decided to keep the same staff in the CCP except for Carol who wanted to work in the RAP. While the rest of the teams were swapped around, the CCP gained a new doctor (from the air force) and a new medic replaced Nico. During the weeks that followed the massacre we had more interviews with the psych team. They seemed to be after statistical data more than anything else. The soldiers soon tired of this and the psych team eventually returned to Australia. They had done their job. Now it was up to each of us to just get on with it. I had taken the opportunity to talk to the psychologist about the bad nightmares and odd flashbacks I had been having since returning from Kibeho. He explained that what I was experiencing was quite normal and would probably decrease as time passed. I tried not to worry too much about it. When the CCP was not at the orphanage the medics worked in the ward to help ease the pressure on medical staff. The best thing about it was we got to see how some of the people we had saved were recovering. Several patients we evacuated from Kibeho were now well enough to go home. The small boy rescued by Jordo would burst into happy laughter each time Jordo entered his room. This boy ended up staying at Mother Teresa's orphanage where Jordo would visit him quite often. Sometimes I would take the boy back to the hospital for lunch and he would wander off looking for Jordo.

The road trips started back up and it was not long until I was picked to go as the medic on one trip to Butare. This was my report:

"On 31 May, 1995 I was the medic allocated as part of a 45-member group of Australian soldiers to attend a day trip to Butare, which is a small town south west of Kigali, the capital of Rwanda. We were going to visit the local cultural museum and we travelled in a four-vehicle convoy all armed with our Steyr rifles, and had American rations to last us the day. We would be travelling via Gitarama, which is west of Kigali. The road from Kigali to Gitarama is designated the 'Red Route' and contra to the briefing I received I found this road to be in reasonable condition. After turning off at Ruhengeri there were no white lines and the road was cratered with many potholes which were so large

that they had to be driven around. All along the edge of the road were hundreds of wrecked vehicles that have been shot up. The road was undulating but we had no problems with United Nations vehicles. Some delays were experienced due to very slow traffic. The distance from Kigali to Gitarama is 56 kilometres and it took us one hour and twenty minutes to travel. While travelling along this road we came to our first roadblock which was directly after the turnoff from Ruhengeri. It was a double roadblock with the ropes being 50 metres apart. There were eight RPA armed soldiers guarding and searching vehicles but they simply waved us through so we were not delayed. About a further three kilometres down the road I noticed a local girl using a hand pump to fill up the typical yellow jerry can with water. It was one of the few functioning water pumps I had seen actually working. Also paralleling this road was a four-strand power line that was still being repaired. We had to cross a long bridge that was guarded by eight RPA fully armed guards who gave us the once over before letting us proceed. There were four at either end of the bridge and they would check every vehicle that crossed. As we progressed further down the road I noticed some quite large areas of gum trees with a fair amount of secondary growth. A lot of the larger trees had been cut down to make charcoal but none of the new growth had been touched. Apparently Australia had sent trees over during the 1950s to help solve the dwindling tree growth. All the way along this road were heaps of children begging in rags, some of them only 500 metres away from a local school. In fact, some children were begging while standing next to, or leaning against three World Food Programme semitrailers which were full of food. How ironic that was. The farming along this road appeared very well organised with the majority of land cultivated with bananas. I noticed a lot of communes (groups of 10 houses together) were unoccupied although some new buildings were being put up. Most of the empty houses used to have people that had either been killed or become internally displaced persons (IDPs), in other words refugees, still in Rwanda. Along the way we overtook 15—20 loaded AHMED semitrailers all heading west loaded with medical stores, and also one International Committee of the Red Cross (ICRC) relief truck. All were heading west to one of the refugee camps. Gitarama was a well organised, reasonably well kept, large township. There were streetlights down the entire length of the main road although I don't know if they actually worked. On the left-hand side of town about one kilometre distance was a very large building with a large red cross which I believe was some form of non-government organisation (NGO). Nearby was also a very large church with all its windows smashed but still structurally sound. A little further down the road was a very large NGO Red Cross presence with at least 10 trucks parked outside a very large fenced compound. Next door to this were three large buildings which had collapsed – whether from explosions or faulty work [or something else] is not known. As had been stated in our briefing there was also the battalion headquarters of the RPA in this town. There was a very large presence of soldiers with at least eight vehicles parked at the local garage some armed with machineguns. There was also a very large RPA compound on the left-hand side of the road as we continued to travel south out of town. This road was designated the 'Yellow Route' and contra to briefings given was in a much better state of repair than the 'Red Route'. It had faded white lines down the middle of the road for most of the distance, and only had very minor potholes here and there which didn't cause us any delay at all. The distance from Gitarama to Butare was about 83 kilometres and it took us about one and a half hours to travel.

"Half way between Gitarama and Butare was a town named Nyanza and there were thousands of local people in one small area just sitting or standing. We could not work out if it was some sort of market but I didn't see any of the normal stalls associated with markets. In this town there were many deserted buildings, even though the buildings that were next door were being extended. In Nyanza was a large NGO presence called Medecins Sans Frontieres which is an international organisation of volunteer doctors and nurses who were, like us, trying to restore Rwanda to some sort of stability. The whole area was well farmed and had power lines for approximately five kilometres although again it wasn't known if these worked. About 10 kilometres short of Butare a civilian vehicle cut in on our leading Land Rover, clipping the bull bar. There was little to no damage to either vehicle however we had a one and a half hour delay while our boss negotiated with the RPA so they would not impound our vehicle. At the bottom of the hill just before entering Butare was yet another RPA roadblock, this one only made of rope strung across the road. Present were three RPA armed soldiers and one local person wearing civilian clothing who was obviously in charge. We were not delayed at all. The museum is a very well kept cultural centre with a large bricked area outside which became a helicopter evacuation landing area during the Kibeho Massacre. The entrance fee was 150 Rwandan Francs (about 50 cents) but we were all happy to pay a US dollar. For an extra cost we could take photos only of things the staff would allow, however one soldier was banned from using a video camera. There was one armed RPA soldier who supervised the staff and advised them what they would be allowed to talk to us about. We spent about 30 minutes inside when the staff decided to close the building. Although the building is quite large we only saw about a quarter of it as we were not permitted to enter certain areas. The whole building had good plumbing and toilet facilities and also a small gift shop. There was a further one and a quarter hour delay as the boss continued to negotiate with the RPA about getting our vehicle back, which eventually happened after many radio communications with our headquarters. During this time I saw ten World Food Programme semitrailers driving past us and taking the turn off to Gikongoro to the west. There were also two ICRC buses going to Butare from the north. All around us were the normal number of children begging and some of them were selling cigarettes at one dollar per packet as well as other trinkets such as watches etc. It was a complete surprise when one of them tried to sell me a French ration pack. At this time we were parked outside the Senegal battalion headquarters awaiting the outcome of the accident investigation. Eventually the negotiations concluded successfully and we were able to begin our return to Kigali. There was little change on the return trip although I did notice that the roadblock just north of Butare was now stopping all vehicles, making people disembark from cars, trucks and buses. All bags and suitcases were completely checked; however we were allowed to proceed unhindered. The return trip was much quicker with less traffic and the same large crowd was still at Nyanza. There were very large areas of gum trees and some pine plantations. The people are generally friendly, including the majority of the RPA. There are large movements of trucks carrying food to all areas of Rwanda, hopefully to the people that need it."

As soon as I got back I typed my report on the computer and handed it in to the CSM. He told me there was no need to write reports on any further trips. I guess by now the intelligence section knew all they had to know.

Work continued at the orphanage every Tuesday and Thursday morning when the CCP ran a medical clinic for the children. There was not a lot for me to do except supervise the setting up of the clinic and allocating tasks, something I quickly grew bored with.

I think what I wanted to do was help the orphanage in other ways. Since Kibeho I had not been able to treat the children. It sounds bad but I didn't want to treat them. I knew that with or without my help they would all either live or die. I had no control over it at all. What I did have control over was being able to fix things in their environment. I knew that if I fixed something that was broken it would stay fixed, and if I could not then it did not really matter. I had total and absolute power over this and it felt much better than having little control over life and death. So I became Mr Fixit.

When one of the nuns asked if I could help her fix a lock on one of the doors I was only too happy to do it. The lock needed replacing so I checked all the doors and found at least another 20 in the same state. I told her I would try to get some new locks. When I later mentioned this to the RSM he suggested that I just take some of the locks off the doors in our accommodation block, so I did – including his. The next time we were at the orphanage I replaced all the locks while the CCP ran the medical clinic. The head sister was pleased and asked if I would look at one of the toilet doors which was rotten and had come off its hinges. I took it off, turned it upside down and reattached it. The next day the sister phoned to tell me some men had tried to break into the building but had left empty-handed because the locks had been fixed. After thanking me, she asked if next time I could look at one of the broken windows. So began a little renovation project that kept me busy while the other members of the CCP team did the clinics.

I asked the engineers if they could put together a small toolkit for me and they were more than happy to oblige. From then on I kept a bag with hammer and nails, screws, chisels, screwdrivers and a tape measure in my vehicle. They even leant me cordless drills. If ever I needed advice about how to fix something I simply checked with the engineers. Among them were qualified plumbers, electricians and carpenters and I learned a lot. One morning I remounted a shelf in a dormitory and one of the novices asked me to take a look at one in the kitchen. The kitchen cooked three meals a day for every one of the 150 people at the orphanage. When I got there I found a small room with two large ovens and two very large cauldrons of boiling water. All the heat was supplied by burning wood. There was food piled on the floor and pots and pans stacked everywhere, leaving very little room to move around and cook. I asked if she would like me make some shelves to make her job easier, and with a huge smile, she said "Yes". So I took measurements of all the walls and drew a plan of where the new shelves would go which she seemed to like. On the way out I noticed the old caretaker, who was about sixty years old, chopping up a massive pile of wood for the kitchen fires. The sisters told me they took turns to chop wood. It took them about four hours a day and the caretaker even longer. Back at the headquarters compound the engineers gave me a stack of leftover sheets of plywood and chipboard as well as a lesson in shelf building. Tim and I spent the next two days putting them together before loading our vehicle and heading back to the orphanage. It took us another day to mount them and when we finished there was no more food or pots and pans left on the floor. One evening in the sergeant's mess I told one of the infantry sergeants about the huge pile of wood the old caretaker and nuns had to chop every day with an axe. He asked if his pioneer section could help. The pioneer section dearly wanted to use their chainsaws, which had not seen much action since arriving in Rwanda. I jumped at the offer and the next morning two pioneer section members cut the whole pile of wood in about three hours. I have never since seen so many smiling faces as I did the moment the caretaker, the sisters and novices saw their wood pile completely cut up.

A variety of different people would come with the CCP to the orphanage, among them the medical company commander, off-duty medics and specialists. Everyone went out of their way to help. When I explained to the transport sergeant about how rocky the orphanage driveway was and how the children would often get hurt when they played there, she told me to put in a request for a bobcat. The request was approved and I was thrilled to escort the bobcat and driver down to the orphanage and watch as he smoothed out the driveway and car park. The children never got cut knees after that.

As well as children, the orphanage also looked after some elderly people and others who could not care for themselves. One man was missing his hands which had been cut off during the genocide the previous year. (Apparently, the perpetrator thought he would not be guilty of murder if the man died because he could not feed himself). This poor man made his way to the orphanage where he was fed by the nuns. He tried to help out by carrying wood to the kitchen in his arms.

One very old lady brought me her old plastic bucket which needed its broken handle fixed. I used coat-hanger wire to fashion a new handle and to make it easier to grip with her arthritic hands and added a smooth wooden handle. She cried when I gave it back to her the next day. Until the day we left Rwanda she never stopped talking about her bucket and proudly showed it to everyone who visited the orphanage, including Ausmed Commander Colonel Walfe. I wonder how many knew it was her bedside bucket for urinating in. I did not dare say a word.

Towards the end of the Rwanda tour we were visited by journalists from Australia. One of them, Ken Kipping, came from Townsville to do a story about our work at the orphanage. My CSM introduced me to Ken and it became my job to take him wherever he needed to go. He interviewed the sisters at the orphanage and took photos of the children. When he returned to Australia he wrote some beautiful stories. I even found several photos of myself in some of his articles. He was a really nice person and was a hit with all the children. I fe t proud to be able to show Ken around and introduce him to the sisters. I wanted to make sure he had a complete understanding of the work the Australian soldiers had done for this orphanage, not only medically but in many other ways.

Another job I was given was to run a first aid course for some of the infantry soldiers who had been to Kibeho and wanted to know more after seeing so much medical work. I started the first course reluctantly, thinking that it would not go all that well, but soon found myself holding a course every second week. I set it up as the equivalent of a St John's Ambulance basic first aid course. I had been a qualified St John's Ambulance instructor for a few years and I contacted the organisation in Australia to see if they would issue their certificates to the soldiers. A week later I received a letter in reply saying they would happily do so at no cost to the soldiers. In no time at all I had run eight courses and more than 50 soldiers had St John's first aid certificates. UNICEF then asked the Ausmed Commander if I could run a course for their staff. Many of them spoke little English so I had to design a test in French, Rwandese and English. Despite a minor glitch when one of the questions had its meaning reversed in translation we succeeded in qualifying 20 of the UNICEF staff in first aid.

As we moved closer to the date of our departure we began packing up the unit to return to Australia. The Defence Force sent over the out-survey team which had the job of packing up everything into shipping containers ready for transportation. With them were members of the customs and immigration department and someone from Australian quarantine. With six weeks left in-country the final group of specialists arrived, including Major Ward, the psychologist who led the psych team that arrived after the Kibeho tragedy. He remained with us until we returned to Australia.

Annual reports were due which meant physical training tests had to be conducted. To prepare I ran laps of the compound to try and maintain a good level of fitness as I had done since arriving in Rwanda. Ten laps were the equivalent of about five kilometres. I had never failed an Army physical training test and I was not about to start now. I ran laps every evening before dinner, sometimes for an hour. I scored 283 out of a possible 300 in the test. Running at an altitude of 2,000 metres around the compound took its toll on my time and I finished the run in twenty minutes instead of my usual eighteen.

We were allowed to run outside the compound but there were restrictions. You could never run alone and you always took a loaded weapon. My friend Andy and I tried to run every day but this was not always possible. Trying to find a running partner could be hard, so it would be back to doing laps of the compound. One day a special forces soldier offered to run with me. I was amused when he turned up carrying a pistol. My personal weapon was the Steyr rifle. He ran a lot faster and I came back from that run completely knackered. While on duty at the hospital I ran on an old treadmill with a mind of its own. It seemed to have three speeds: fast, really fast and dead stop. I could run at a good pace for an hour or so, but when it came time to get off I had to leap into the air and land with my feet on either side of the machine. Try and stop it by turning it off and you risked being spat out of the room. Once it nearly threw me out the window!

Occasionally I worked in the ward for a few days. The second-in-charge of the UNAMIR mission needed some minor surgery and when he arrived I volunteered to look after him. A Ghanaian, whose UN vehicle number was seven, was thrilled when I admitted him to Room 7 because the number held special significance for him. It was a complete fluke but I kept him happy by making sure he was discharged seven days after being admitted and booking him for an out-patients appointment seven days later. Unaware that I had done it on purpose, he was ecstatic by the time he left the hospital. When he returned for his appointment he brought his female Army corporal cook with him. He explained that because it had been such a lucky stay, and I had looked after him so well, I was now able to marry this girl. She was his gift to me. I thanked him for his kind thought and spent nearly 10 minutes explaining to him why it was not necessary and that I was already married. For the next fortnight I tried to live the incident down as my fellow sergeants sent me anonymous wedding invitations, the odd bunch of flowers and even a set of divorce papers.

Our packing went up a gear with only four weeks until the mission ended. Customs and quarantine went through everything, advising what we could take back to Australia and what had to be left behind. Some of the hospital equipment had to stay so the Australian government donated nearly $10 million worth to the Kigali hospital, including beds and X-ray and theatre equipment. I donated most of the remaining medical stores to the Rwandan hospital and the orphanage and took truckload after truckload to them.

Quarantine officials advised that anyone who had worked in Kibeho would have to burn all their field equipment because of the danger of contamination by cholera and other diseases. The only thing I managed to save was my knife because I was able to sterilise it. As all soldiers know, losing your webbing is like losing a really close friend. The rest of my non-essential gear was packed into my trunk, checked by customs, sealed and then stored to await transport to Australia.

Resus duties continued and on one occasion I was called to Resus B which was expecting two casualties. I was a little bewildered when the rest of team Bravo began putting on white plastic protective overalls and plastic see-through masks. I had worked in Kibeho and had not even been issued any of that stuff. I really could not see the point in any of it. I put the overalls on, even though I did not want to, but did not bother with the mask. There was bugger-all wrong with the casualties anyway. It all seemed like overkill to me. On my last Resus A duty a small girl was brought in with head injuries caused by her house collapsing on her. Instead of being the scribe on this resus, I was the medic. When it came time to inject a drug into the drip I got the shakes really badly. There was nothing I could do to stop my hands from shaking. The air force doctor working with me would not come near me for fear of being stabbed with the needle and it took all my strength just to settle my hands so I could finally administer the drugs. The doctor wanted to take over from me but I would not let her because I really felt I needed to get over my problem. It had nothing to do with the patient or the pressure of doing the resuscitation. I was having a series of flashbacks that had plagued me since Kibeho. Flashing before my eyes were images of me putting in drips and administering morphine to all those horrifically wounded people. It was quite nerve-racking. Major Mary Brandy again came to the rescue by talking me through the whole thing. The air force doctor had very little sympathy and seemed to think I was just a dickhead. When the resus was over Mary Brandy stayed with me as I explained what had happened. Thankfully it was the last resus duty I did in Rwanda.

As we gradually wound down the mission I worked furiously to complete any remaining handyman tasks at the orphanage. As different sections in the hospital began to close down some of the staff pitched in to help me. Even the specialist medical staff would come along and put up shelving in the dormitories. Packages of medical stores would be delivered day and night along with leftover rations from our kitchen. As the soldiers cleaned out the barracks they asked if the orphanage could find a use for items like furniture, fridges and mattresses. One day I delivered 50 mattresses to the orphanage, much to the amazement of the nuns. There were so many the nuns sent some to other orphanages in the country. A large fridge was especially welcome because they did not have one.

With just a few days to go some of us bought Rwandan flags to take back to Australia as souvenirs. The RPA were not impressed by this and advised that anyone caught selling flags would be punished and anyone caught with a flag would have it confiscated. I bought two and folded one of them until it fitted into an empty water bottle. The other one I wrapped around my waist just before the RPA searched our gear as we were about to board the plane to Australia. The Canadian contingent and Care Australia held a huge party to farewell the Australian contingent with loud music and plenty of beer. In his speech the force commander congratulated us all on a job well done. The next day the barracks had a final clean and inspection before being handed over to the RPA. During some of the more boring times I had drawn African animals on my wardrobe doors with a black marker pen. One of the RPA officers told me my art was graffiti and I must scrape my metal wardrobe doors clean. After scrubbing the doors with steel wool for several hours I decided it was easier to paint them instead.

Two days before we left, the orphanage held a party for us. Even the Ausmed Commander and our Commanding Officer attended. The children put on a beautiful display of African dancing and music and served some African food. Jordo's little mate decided this was the best time to ask if he could go back to Australia with him. We all knew it was not possible. The only thing Jordo could say was he would see what he could do. While putting up the last new shelf in the kitchen I ran out of battery power in the drill. I explained to the caretaker how he could do it with nails instead. We said goodbye to all the children and nuns and went back to the barracks for our final night in Rwanda. I was excited about going home and did not sleep much.

The Canadian contingent drove us to the airport where we had our final customs and immigration checks. A Rwandan official insisted on checking every bag and trunk. Remembering the flag I had hidden in the water bottle, I placed an Army book on top of all the gear in my trunk. When it was opened up the official was more interested in looking at the book and made only a token search. After a three-hour wait, my two flags and I boarded the plane, nicknamed *Freedom Bird*, for the return journey to Australia.

Chapter Nine

Home from hell

"In the meantime life at home had become a little rough. I had been having nightmares about Kibeho since about two weeks after the event and they were still troubling me. I also found my patience was wearing thin very quickly. Little things would annoy me and a lot of the time I felt intensely frustrated."

As the plane left the ground a mighty cheer erupted from every soldier, sailor and airman that shook the very bolts of the airframe. But getting back to Australia was not without its dramas. We refuelled at Mauritius, a small island off the east coast of Africa, but were not allowed to get off the plane despite a long delay. All the doors were opened to allow in some fresh air meaning we could only sit and watch when fuel was accidentally spilled all over the wings. That meant a wait of another hour for the fuel to evaporate before we could take off. At Singapore we were allowed off the plane and headed to the small airport smoking lounge to get in as many cigarettes as we could before the next leg to Perth.

Another huge cheer shook the plane when we touched down in Perth. We were finally in Australia again and it felt really good to be back on home soil. Only the soldiers who hailed from Perth were annoyed. They were less than 10 kilometres from their homes but still had to fly through to Townsville for our medal parade. After waiting another hour it was back on the plane for the final leg. We arrived in Townsville in the late afternoon. A lot of families were there to greet their husbands, wives, brothers or sisters, including mine. At a very quick parade in the terminal each member of the contingent received an Australian Service medal, still in the box and not to be worn until presented at the medal parade the next day at Lavarack Barracks. Buses took us to the barracks where we spent a couple of hours sorting out bags and trunks. As the medical company representative of the Regimental Trust Fund I also had to sort out the issue of plaques and other items for the medical company members. This meant less time with my family who had booked into one of the local motels.

The medal parade was called forward because some people had to fly out first thing in the morning. In a large hall we all formed up in company groups, standing shoulder to shoulder, to be presented with our Australian Service medals. A local politician gave a speech praising our efforts in Rwanda, particularly those present during the Kibeho massacre. We took our newly issued and very shiny Australian Service Medals out of our pockets and waited for whoever was pinning them onto our shirts. The contingent RSM Alan Castle pinned on mine. We mingled after the parade and I was able to sit and spend a little time catching up with Nico who was still unable to walk because of the injuries he sustained in the accident. Afterwards I went back to issuing plaques to the medical company soldiers. My family and I managed to get to the motel by about eleven that night. I kept thinking: *Well that's it; it's all over and finished. What the hell am I going to do now?*

The bloke next door asked if I wanted a beer. We ended up sitting quietly in the gutter, drinking a couple of Fourex beers and smoking before I decided to try and get some sleep. They were probably the best two beers I have ever tasted.

The next morning my family and I went to the RAAF base to catch the air force plane back to Brisbane. Some soldiers booked their own flights because the RAAF plane, although free, was going to Brisbane and then on to Melbourne, Adelaide and Sydney where it would arrive late that night. They simply could not wait to get home. We flew to Amberley air base, near Ipswich, where we caught a minibus to Enoggera barracks. Tara's mother picked us up from just inside the front gate and drove us home. After reporting into my unit and handing in all my documents, I had five weeks of leave which I mainly spent getting to know Kelsey and Alanna again. I started running properly again, stopped smoking and generally just relaxed before starting back at work back at 2nd/14th Light Horse Regiment (2/14 LHR) RAP. Looking back I can say that during that leave period I was restless and a little bored. I was looking forward to working again.

A couple of weeks after returning to work the sergeant's mess held a mixed formal dining-in night. A lot of my sergeant mates asked me how Rwanda had been. I told them that it had been a good experience both as a medic and as a soldier. I did not say anything about Kibeho. I did not think anyone would be that interested, and besides I did not like talking about it after what happened to my company commander during the first debrief. One sergeant commented on my medals, saying it was typical that hard workers from the Armoured Corps like himself never got a chance to go overseas, unlike medics like me. I was a bit dumb-founded by the comments but I tried to take it in my stride.

A few days later I was on my way to the sergeant's mess for morning tea when I ran into one of the quartermaster store warrant officers. The first thing he said was, "Welcome back... and did you have a good holiday?" Annoyed that he was talking about the tour to Rwanda in a smart-arse way, I replied that the holiday I had while I was on leave was great. He apologised because he knew how such comments could hurt. He had served in Somalia and no doubt the same sort of thing happened to him. Many soldiers returning from overseas get similar comments and we had been warned it would occur. There was a certain amount of jealousy felt by some soldiers who had not been overseas, particularly as I was seen as "just a medic" and not a "real soldier".

A couple of months later I was asked to give the whole regiment a presentation about what I had done during the mission in Rwanda. Three of us took part: an Armoured Corps sergeant, a legal officer from the first contingent, and me from the second contingent. I contacted army public relations in Canberra to get hold of some slides and arranged my presentation around these. It all went well until I got to the part about Kibeho. I really struggled to try and explain what had happened over there and the horror of it all. It was difficult but I eventually got through it. There were a lot of questions that I managed to answer and when it was all over some of the officers and sergeants thanked me for an excellent presentation. It was only later that the RSM pulled me aside and quietly told me he thought I should seek some professional help or counselling. After the presentation I presented the club PMC (president of the mess committee) with one of the Rwandan flags I had smuggled out of the country. There was a tradition that anyone from the unit who went overseas was to bring a flag back. The whole ceiling of the boozer was covered with different flags.

Back to work I went, but the only thing that really held my interest was increasing my physical training even more. I ran to and from work. At lunchtime I played touch football. I finished sixth in the unit cross country, coming first in my age group. I had no trouble passing the physical training test, scoring 298 points out of a possible 300. But I failed to crack the 18-minute mark for the five-kilometre run and that disappointed me. So I trained harder. I began running three times a day as hard as I could. I also did gym sessions and weight training until I realised that maybe my days of sub-18 five-kilometre runs were probably over. After all I was now 36 years old.

One day I received a letter from Alanna's class at school asking me to visit them to talk about my service in Rwanda. I wore my medals and the blue UN beret. It was fun to talk to the kids because I had kept in contact with the whole class by sending letters and postcards while I was overseas. The seven-year-olds asked plenty of questions and I thought I managed to answer all of them quite well. The boys in particular asked things like, "Did you kill anyone?", "Did anyone die?' and "Did you have a gun?" I answered these questions as simply as possible.

Several weeks later the RSM called the whole unit on parade and I was told I had to attend. Usually I would get out of these parades citing work commitments but this time I reluctantly attended. To my amazement, the divisional commander of 1st Division presented me with the Land

Commander's Commendation in recognition of my contributions to the medical support force in Rwanda, particularly in Kibeho. However, my pride went a little flat when one of the other sergeants was awarded a Brigade Commander's Commendation for performing outstanding work as the orderly room chief clerk.

In the meantime life at home had become a little rough. I had been having nightmares about Kibeho since about two weeks after the event and they were still troubling me. I also found my patience was wearing thin very quickly. Little things would annoy me and a lot of the time I felt intensely frustrated. I did not seem to be able to move forward in life. I was not really enjoying things as I should be. I could not concentrate and would occasionally get lost when I was driving. Sometimes I would forget where I was going. I was due for a posting in a couple of weeks and was hoping it would all settle down. After all I had been told that this kind of thing was quite normal for someone who had just returned from overseas. The thing was I could not remember it happening to me when I returned from my three-month tour of duty in Malaysia.

A week before I was due to be transferred to 8th/9th Battalion, Royal Australian Regiment (8/9RAR), I was promoted to staff sergeant. I believed I was finally ready to move forward again. I was also going to fulfil one of my greatest ambitions – becoming medical platoon commander of the medical platoon in 8/9RAR. The new sergeant medical assistant marched into 2/14 LHR for a smooth two-day handover and then I was out of there. I marched into 8/9RAR in November 1995, worked for one week and then went on Christmas leave.

I spent the next 12 months working hard at 8/9RAR. I was responsible for the whole unit on the medical level. I had all the medical files brought up to date and organised ongoing medical training for the RAP staff. Brett Dale was the medical sergeant and we worked closely together to ensure our medics had the best possible training, getting them on as many courses as we could. The year flew but I never felt quite right within myself. Eventually I went to our unit doctor and was referred to a psychiatrist who diagnosed me with post-traumatic stress disorder (PTSD) as a result of my experiences in Rwanda. The brigade senior medical officer and brigade commander approved nine days' sick leave and I went to my brother's house in Townsville to get away from it all. When I got back to Brisbane I was asked to go to Sydney with some others who had been in Kibeho and to write a statement. I was still unaware it would be used to help decide nominations of honours and awards. I provided a statement virtually identical to the one I gave my commanding officer in Rwanda. The leader of the whole Australian Army spoke to us and said our work in Kibeho would not go unrecognised, but when he asked if anyone was having any problems I wasn't game to say anything. My heart was racing and my nerves were shot, but I could not admit I was suffering PTSD, especially in front of all the other blokes who seemed fine.

I threw myself back into work. Brett and I ran a patrol medic's course – a first for the unit and the whole of 6th Brigade. It was a great success and when the brigade was short a doctor to go to Brunei with Alpha Company 8/9RAR for a month, I went. It was hard work trudging through the jungles of Borneo but I loved it and the time in barracks was more like a holiday. It was a good break from home and normal unit activities. I also managed to give a half-decent presentation about my experiences in Rwanda.

I had a few more weeks of work back at 8/9RAR before going on annual Christmas leave at the end of November. In the New Year the unit geared up for a brigade exercise near Woomera in central Australia. I was looking forward to it and had all the medics packing and ordering extra medical supplies. All went well until one night at home I completely lost the plot.

Above. Some of the younger orphans at Mother Teresa's orphanage. Most are under two years old. This orphanage looked after 118 orphans.

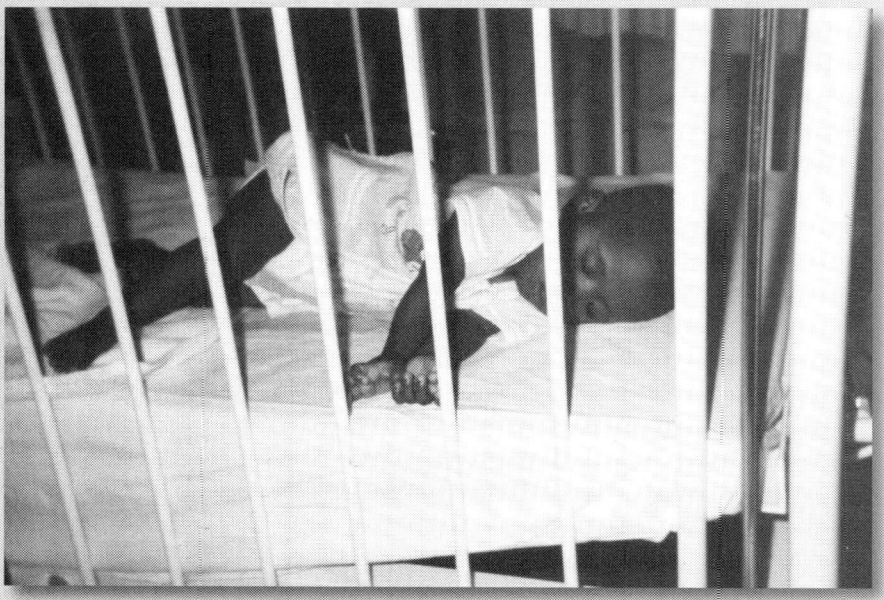

Above. Tiny three year old girl, Miss Nyonsaba, put in Ausmed hospital with tuberculosis.

Above. This is Nyirayabimana with me. This eleven year old girl had suffered machete blows to the head in 1994. She was dragged out of her house and struck twice across the head. She played dead until the attackers left and then hid in the local dump before her brother found her. The top scar covers a missing section of bone in her head where you could see her brain pulsating with each heart beat. She was in hospital to have this surgically repaired by replacing the missing part of her skull with bone from her hip.

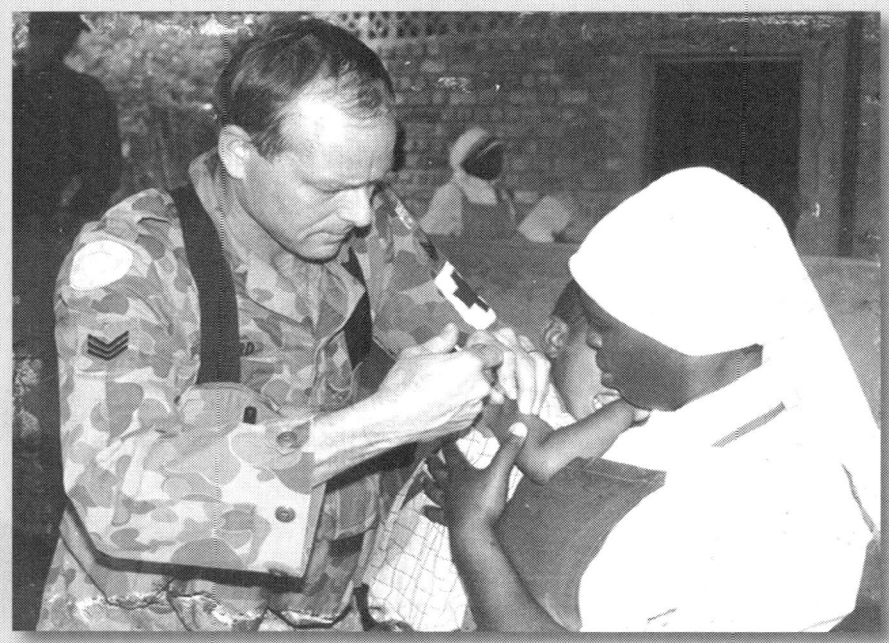

Above. The CCP ran an immunisation programme for all the children.

Above. The land rover and trailer used by me parked in front of Mother Teresa's orphanage. It was also used by the CCP during the Kibeho Massacre.

Left. Me sitting with one of the orphans from Mother Teresa's who just had a large abscess drained from his head.

Above. Even with a large presence of RPA and UN soldiers a man removed the number plates from this shot up VW Kombi and placed them on his own Mazda 626.

Above. The kids from CARE Australia orphanage enjoy a day out and a visit from the Easter bunny loaded with chocolate eggs.

Left. Me as the Easter bunny ready to visit the orphans.

Above. This bike made of wood did 30 kilometres per hour downhill while the child carried a bag of coal on his or her head.

Above. The mug I found in the first location used for the CCP. I had it engraved with all the names of the Australian soldiers present during the Kibeho tragedy. The navy dental assistant kindly went through a few of drill bits to do the job. Each Anzac Day I drink a rum and coke from the mug to remember my time in Rwanda.

Above. The medals I have been awarded during my army career. From left: AASM for Rwanda, ASM for service in S.E. Asia, DFSM for fifteen years' or more service, ADM for military service and the UN medal with Rwanda ribbon for service with the United Nations.

Above. Three mates, Ken Pickard, Terry Pickard and Milan Nikolic in Brisbane on my wedding day, 2006.

Commendation

49784 Sergeant Terence Robert Pickard

Royal Australian Army Medical Corps

Australian Contingent

United Nations Assistance Mission for Rwanda

Your Commanding Officer has brought to my attention your exceptional and dedicated devotion to duty while serving with the Australian Medical Support Force in Rwanda. Your tireless efforts at Kibeho, under appalling and dangerous conditions, were instrumental in saving many lives. In addition, your coordination of the health support tasks in support of Mother Theresa's orphanage in Kigali ensured a lasting and positive legacy of Australia in the hearts of the children and the nuns caring for them.

Your efforts have brought great credit upon yourself, the Royal Australian Army Medical Corps and the Australian Army.

P.M. ARNISON
Major General
Land Commander Australia

31 October 1995

Above. I was awarded the Land Commander's Commendation for my efforts in Kibeho and for the work I did with Mother Teresa's orphanage. Four of the soldiers were awarded with the Medal Of Gallantry including Lieutenant Tilbrook, Captain Carol Vaughan-Evens and two others. A couple of other minor awards were given to soldiers who were in Kibeho as well. Unfortunately Jordo, Nico, Tim, and Churchy were not amongst them. I believe that each person should have been awarded something in recognition for their outstanding efforts in Kibeho, perhaps a group bravery award.

Chapter Ten

Losing
the plot

"Nothing felt right. It was as though I was floating along, completely disassociated from the rest of the world. I could not focus on anything and conversation seemed distant and trivial. I went to the military hospital and told the doctor in casualty that I thought I was suffering the effects of post-traumatic stress disorder. They admitted me and the next day I was transferred to New Farm clinic."

One evening I was having a few beers with my brother Ken and struggling to get images of the Kibeho Massacre out of my mind. It was terrible. We were talking about the times we had spent overseas and I was trying to describe Kibeho and the atrocities I had witnessed. For some reason I felt I could not make him understand how terrible I was feeling. I wrongly thought that a bottle of whisky, on top of the beers I had already consumed, might help me explain it better. But it seemed no matter how much I drank or how much I talked, I could not make him realise how much I was struggling to live my life each day with this mess of emotions bottled up inside me. I went to work the next morning but it was impossible to function normally. It was not just the bad hangover that was making me feel as if I had no interest in living, let alone working. All I could do was doze on the bed in the treatment room. When I got home nothing felt right. It was as though I was floating along, completely disassociated from the rest of the world. I could not focus on anything and conversation seemed distant and trivial. I went to the military hospital and told the doctor in casualty that I thought I was suffering the effects of post-traumatic stress disorder (PTSD). They admitted me and the next day I was transferred to New Farm clinic.

To explain how I got to that point I have to go back a few steps and describe in more detail how my mind was working at that time. I had read all the information packages and booklets I had been issued on post-traumatic stress, but I believe it does not matter how well informed you are, you will not know how ill you are until someone else tells you. Some sufferers react by going on a life-long drinking binge or driving like maniacs. Left untreated, post-traumatic stress can cause all sorts of character-altering behaviour. Unfortunately, it can also have a devastating effect on the people around you. When I look back now it's obvious that I was exhibiting signs and symptoms of PTSD for at least a year without knowing it. As an army medic I was used to watching and treating other people. I rarely took much interest in my own mental well-being. There used to be a stigma attached to soldiers suffering PTSD, for example World War I soldiers whose shell-shock was mistakenly assumed to be cowardice, often ended with them being shot. Even nowadays when we are better informed it can be quite difficult to talk about. Just admitting the problem is hard. Understanding the problem might be harder if you have not been there yourself. It is felt so badly by some veterans that they give up all hope and commit suicide.

When I returned from Rwanda I had about a month off and assumed that would be enough time for me to get back on an even keel. I ran to and from work. Even while I was on leave I ran for at least an hour a day. It was how I kept fit and I enjoyed it. I also felt a need to run at lunch-time, and if it was quiet work out at the gymnasium. At home I exercised continuously. I felt I was achieving nothing if I did not. This "need" for exercise is a classic sign of PTSD. I felt I had to prove something. I could not prove myself to anyone else, so I was trying to prove myself to me.

When I was asked to give a presentation to the unit about Rwanda it took me a couple of weeks to set up. After all my work organising things like photos and slides from Canberra and maps from the intelligence section, I became angry when the talk was delayed for a week. I just could not understand why soldiers in the unit did not think my presentation was important. I believed that no matter how I felt about Rwanda it just didn't seem important enough for anyone else to listen to. In fact, something else had taken priority over the presentation, but the CO at the time did not want to cancel my talk and postponed it for a week. Anger, frustration and a feeling of not being in control is another symptom of PTSD.

I had the feeling during my presentation that I was failing to get my thoughts across just as I had when I was talking to my brother. It all went well until I spoke about Kibeho and my manner changed. I started talking very loud and fast. I was not aware of it at the time. It was as if I could not tell them enough, or emphasise the horror enough in the short time I had to speak. I could not seem to get across the importance of it all. When I finished several officers and warrant officers thanked me for my presentation. The RSM did the same but also advised me that he thought I needed help dealing with the mental trauma. Of course, I thought everything would be fine. I did not realise how manic I had seemed during the talk, although I was aware that my heart rate had risen and I was breathing a lot faster than normal.

I did however take the RSM's advice and visited the psych unit, located in the Brisbane suburb of Kelvin Grove, which supported Enoggera Barracks. When I got there I bumped into one of the army reserve cooks who had been in Rwanda at the same time as me. He was also having some trouble. I remember thinking that if he was struggling then perhaps I needed some professional help because he was lucky enough not to have confronted the worst of it. After filling out a lot of paperwork, I saw a psychologist who simply advised me that each time I thought about Kibeho I should try and imagine a stop sign. This would help get rid of the bad thoughts and allow me to carry on with what I was doing. I tried this while driving back to the unit and nearly crashed the Land Rover. Loss of concentration is another sign of PTSD. Once I was heading towards Yeronga, a suburb on the south side of Brisbane, but then I realised I was actually halfway to Greenbank rifle range instead.

Eventually I made an appointment with Dr Malcolm Foxcroft, the visiting psychiatrist for the Army, at the military hospital at Yeronga. He told me I had PTSD and prescribed some medication but it made me feel so ill that a week later I stopped taking it. I did not know that most anti-depressants take around two weeks to adjust to. It was during that week that I went to Sydney to write my statement about Kibeho. When the commander of the Australian Army, Major General Peter Arnison addressed us he asked if anyone had any problems due to serving in Rwanda and at Kibeho. I was not game enough to say anything, especially since the other five sitting with me seemed fine. Not being able to fully recognise your own signs and symptoms is one of the major problems with having PTSD.

When I joined 8/9RAR and handed my documents into the orderly room a sergeant commented that I was just one of those medics lucky enough to have scored an overseas holiday and get a medal for it. It took all my self-control not to hit him. I was so angry. He had no idea how hurtful that remark was. I stormed off to the RAP to meet the blokes and basically worked for a week before going on leave. But I left with a lot of pent-up anger simmering away inside me that I could not get rid of.

On the home front I found that everything was annoying me. Little everyday things would frustrate and anger me. When my daughter Alanna refused to eat I would yell that if she was hungry enough she would eat the corn out of pieces of shit. I told her to just eat or I would belt her. I never did – it was my anger and frustration talking and it was no good to anyone. When little Kelsey fell over and grazed her knee it took me ages to do anything about it. When I got round to treating her, I told her: "Stop your whingeing, your injury is nothing. I have seen people walking around with half their chest missing and they survived. I am sure that you will survive too."

145

I could not seem to communicate with my wife. In a way I did not want to because I knew she could not comprehend what I was struggling with. Her response was usually along the lines of "You'll be right", "Just get over it", "It's all in the past" or "Just move on". But for me it wasn't in the past. I was having nightmares nearly every night and flashbacks several times a day. I could not concentrate at work. Luckily as staff sergeant in charge I could just task everyone else to do the work. I had an excellent sergeant in Brett Dale and he ran most of the RAP for me while I looked after the administration. But although Kibeho was now well over a year ago, for me it continued to happen every single day and night. And I had no idea what to do about it.

I couldn't stand anyone who did not appear genuinely ill and wanted to see the doctor during sick parade. I would go out into the waiting room, sift through the waiting soldiers and tell those that I thought were having a bludge to leave. That is not necessarily a bad thing but when you start telling sick soldiers to leave that's when trouble starts. Luckily Brett knew this was happening and suggested I do more of the office work while he took charge of the medical side of things.

When I first arrived at 8/9RAR I could not handle doing any medical procedures. After working with limited supplies in Rwanda, I could not see the reason for doing treatments that took so long. I had seen people with horrendous injuries survive with minimal treatment and limited sterilisation, sometimes without any form of pain relief. What we were doing in our treatment room now seemed like overkill to me. Treating our soldiers' injuries any differently seemed like a waste of time, effort and resources. It was best that I avoided all medical work.

I still loved going out in the field, away from my family and the unit's barrack environment. I was able to work alone and make all the medical decisions myself without question, just like I had in Rwanda. I did not have to worry about what to me seemed the trivial things in life. Out in the field I found some peace being by myself, but I also started to have some huge arguments with other sergeants. Field training appeared to be the most important thing in their lives, but to me it was nothing special. It was all just training. None of it felt like the real thing anymore. I simply assumed they were less qualified because they had not been in the situations I had. I still carried out my duties but they felt mundane, pointless and boring.

Some things I could not get enough of. I loved computers and would draw up tables and graphs of statistics for the company commander on how much work the medical staff was doing. He soon got sick of this and sent a message down via the CSM that he knew how hard the medical platoon worked and he did not need pie graphs every day to remind him. I stopped doing it, but wondered why nobody appeared interested in our work.

I put my staff under enormous pressure to get extra training. I got them to attend as many courses as possible and then nominated them for promotion once they qualified. I also felt the need to put myself under pressure by running courses, instructing, doing weapons training and physical training. It was as if I needed to be under the type of stress I had been exposed to in Rwanda and I was running myself into the ground.

At home I was finding looking after my children extremely frustrating. The orphanage at Kigali had shown me that no matter how someone was brought up they could still survive and reach adulthood. I had begun not to care how my children were brought up and had little concern for them. I was having enough trouble of my own. Nobody knew what the hell was going on and it was driving them crazy. I visited my medical officer and told him I was having terrible nightmares and not enjoying being home with my family. He suggested I take some stress leave and go away for a few days. This was how I came to be in Townsville with my brother Ken. During my nine-day stay I tried to quell the nightmares with beer but it did not help. In fact, the dreams seemed to get worse. They all related to the helplessness of treating multiple casualties and me watching on as they disintegrated into unrecognisable corpses. The corpses usually became my own children who somehow survived despite horrific injuries. In the dreams I could not work out why they were still alive. The darkest moments in the nightmares came when I wished they would just hurry up and die. I would wake up in a panic, covered in sweat and too scared to go back to sleep. I lay awake until daylight when it felt safer and then tried to sleep a little more.

The break did nothing to help my focus at work and I finally decided it was time I saw someone other than a psychologist. My medical officer referred me back to Dr Foxcroft. Once again I could only take the medication for a week before the side effects made me quit.

Despite being told I had PTSD I could not grasp why I was feeling so bad and prone to fits of anger. At any time of the day or night a smell, sound or sight could set off a flashback. I had no control over it. I could not even sit down and read a book. My nightmares were so real I thought I was actually there and the flashbacks would instantly take me back. It was just Kibeho, Kibeho, Kibeho. My life revolved around the place and I was not even there.

I also struggled to understand why I was having such a hard time when it seemed nobody else was. The battalion second-in-charge, Major McCrohan, never mentioned anything about having difficulties. When Jon Church dropped into the battalion RAP for a visit he told me he never had nightmares. Carol Vaughan-Evans was another who said she had no problems. The blokes I met in Sydney when I went to see the Land Commander seemed all right. So why was I the only one? I started to feel very alone and disappointed that I could not control my mind. I started to wonder if I was losing the plot.

A week after I saw Churchy he was tragically killed in a Blackhawk helicopter crash during an exercise in Townsville. Seventeen other soldiers were also killed. It sent me into a bit of a spin. I began thinking that everything I did was no longer worth it if life could end so abruptly. Dr Foxcroft helped me get through this rough period and I was able to push on. Beer helped me sleep without dreaming, but not always.

At one stage I decided that since I knew so much about trauma – and had treated so many different injuries in Rwanda – I should be a doctor. I rang every university in Australia to find out how to go about this but soon gave up because the process seemed too hard.

In the middle of the year, four of the soldiers at Kibeho were awarded the Gallantry Medal. I felt let down that the rest of us did not receive anything in recognition for what we had achieved. I had been awarded the Land Commander's Commendation but the same award can be given to a clerk for doing a good job without even leaving Australia. I had nominated my two corporals, Tim Whyte and Milan Nikolic for the Nursing Services Cross, but it went to an operating theatre sister because he had served in Cambodia and Rwanda. He never even went to Kibeho. I was angry. Why was there no group bravery award? Whatever happened to the possibility of a unit citation? Why were we not being recognised? My anger was getting hard to control.

Running, working, drinking, dreaming...it was all coming to a head. My sense of embarrassment was growing as I struggled to talk about it. Then, as I tried to get it all out with Ken, I drank that bottle of scotch. That was the end of my military career. That was the end of my family life. In fact, it was the end of my life as I knew it.

It tipped me over the edge. The next morning I knew something was seriously wrong. I had faced stressful situations before and had been able to handle them. I had always been in control. I knew my strengths and weaknesses. But now I was completely out of my league. I had lost the plot. All day I felt emotionally dead. At that moment I could see no reason to be alive. I could not take any more. Luckily, I knew enough to get to the hospital.

I told the nursing officer I thought I was suffering from PTSD and had to see a doctor. He admitted me straight away, gave me sleeping tablets and put me in isolation. I refused any visitors. I could not face anyone and I did not want to have to explain my emotional state of mind. I just wanted to shut my brain down and sleep the rest of my life away. The next day I was transferred to New Farm clinic, the Army's preferred medical facility for psychiatric patients. My whole life was about to change.

Chapter Eleven

19 years, 74 days

"I was going to be discharged, medically unfit for service due to PTSD, the result of my service in Rwanda and at Kibeho. There was no farewell for me when I left the Army. My life had changed drastically and somehow I was going to have to learn to live with my mental illness."

I was admitted to New Farm clinic and shown around before being taken to my own room. As soon as I saw the bed I lay down and tried to go to sleep. No sooner had I done that than Rosie, one of the enrolled nurses, started the admission procedures. I struggled to stay awake as she asked the usual questions such as name, age and weight. She was very kind but I just wanted to close my eyes. A few minutes later I was hit by spasms of diarrhoea which kept me stuck in the toilet for the next hour. I was placed on some heavy sedation and left alone until Dr Malcolm Foxcroft could see me the next morning. During the night I awoke repeatedly soaked in sweat from my nightmares.

In the morning I managed to make my way down to the dining hall for breakfast, but I could not eat. I sat at a table by myself not knowing anyone and wondering what the hell was going to happen. As I looked around I saw men, women and even young teenage girls. I wondered if they were all psychiatrically ill. I felt very alone as I watched a lady playing the piano and another singing. I quickly drank my coffee before going back to my room to get some more sleep. I was physically and mentally exhausted.

One of the sisters took me to get weighed. I staggered down the hall to the scales in the bathroom. The sedation from the night before had still not worn off. When I returned to my room the sister sat with me and asked how I was. I did not know what to say so I started talking about what I was feeling. I told her I thought I was suffering from PTSD. When I started to explain about the trauma I had seen in Kibeho, I was amazed that she said nothing. She just let me talk. I talked about all the injured I treated, how I felt this overwhelming guilt about not being able to do anything as I watched so many people get slaughtered, and about how I had to triage the injured. I rambled on while she just sat there, making a small comment now and then but never interrupting me. It was the first time I was able to talk about things that way. She stayed with me for more than an hour before I fell asleep again.

Later in the morning Dr Foxcroft turned up to talk to me. He advised me that I would probably be in hospital for a while and that I needed to start some anti-depressant medication. I was not keen, especially since the previous time they had made me feel so sick, but now I really did not care about anything. I just wanted to get my mind back and I thought that sleep would do this. I started the medication and slowly descended into a very dark place in my mind as I tried to cope with everything I was trying to hide

151

or get rid of. I wanted to make the visions and memories of Kibeho, so real and fresh, just disappear. But I could not do it without making everything else disappear as well. So I just gave in, let it all go and remained focused just enough to stay alive. In the first couple of weeks I did little else apart from eat, drink and go to the toilet. I rarely showered and hardly shaved. I had no interest in anything except survival.

During those first couple of weeks, I received a few phone calls from people I knew really well. But when I answered the phone I could not remember who they were. Apparently I would say, "I am sorry but I don't know who you are", and then hang up. One of the calls was from a close friend and partner of my mother-in-law, Chris. It was very upsetting for me as they tried to explain who they were, but no matter what they said I just could not work it out. Eventually the nurses stopped putting phone calls through to me. When my unit Padre visited I had no idea who he was and could only sit and listen to what he said without really understanding him. I had known him very well for a couple of years but I recall sitting dumbfounded as I tried to remember who he was until I was so frustrated I asked him to leave. After he left the nurses told me who he was.

Someone I did recognise was Major McCrohan, now the 8th/9th Battalion second-in-command. He had some understanding of what I was going through. He told me that since coming back from Rwanda he had struggled with certain issues, particularly with his children. I wondered why he had never said anything about it before. But at least it was good to know someone else felt the same way and I was not alone. That was the first time I ever heard anyone apart from me admit that they had some issues resulting from Kibeho.

Dr Malcolm Foxcroft visited every morning to check how I was going and to adjust my medication. One morning I told him that when the leaves blew across the courtyard all I could see was rats. I could also hear the leaves moving from one side of the courtyard to the other. He explained that I was hyper-sensitive and hyper-vigilant but added valium to my medication to help. I really did not care what he did. I just wanted to stop seeing the rats. I was encouraged to attend classes on anger management and how to change your belief systems. I went but found it hard to absorb anything. I just sat in the chair like a zombie. I had no interest in anything around me. I just wanted to hide within myself. The lessons were three times a day and lasted an hour each. In between I slept in my room until a nurse woke me up to tell me I had to go to class. There were times when I was too sick to attend so Malcolm gave me permission not to go and I would sleep the day away. Even in my stupor I tried hard to go to the lessons because I knew just being there might help. I was desperate to try and get at least some of my mind back and I did not care how.

My wife came to visit with Kelsey and Alanna and we went to the park. I was still focused on my own internal battle and had little to say. We went to the shops and the local park to have a look around and I barely made it back to the clinic. I slept for the rest of the day. It was as if they had never been. Members of my unit visited me but I have no memory of them being there. As the medication started to take effect and I got used to it, I slowly began to take a little more interest in my surroundings. Some days I sat in the courtyard watching the other patients. Some were bi-polar and in hospital to try new medication. There was a group of teenage girls suffering from anorexia. Like me they were all trying to get home. From what I could see mental illness was highly treatable. Maybe there was some hope for me.

I improved as the weeks passed. I started to come out of the dark place at the bottom of my mind and began shaving and showering every day. *I must be getting better*, I thought to myself. I began talking to other patients but was always careful to avoid mentioning Kibeho because the medical staff thought it might be too disturbing. I found this hard to do as I listened to other patients discuss their illnesses.

Just when I felt there was some light at the end of the tunnel, I was hit by two body blows. The first was the end of my marriage. Tara and I decided we could no longer be together. It was an emotional and painful moment in my life. I was a completely different person since being in Rwanda and not the same person I had been before I left. We could no longer get on. The second setback was when Malcolm told me I was probably going to be discharged from the Army. I took another tumble down the dark hole for a couple of weeks. In the clinic's courtyard, under some very heavy sedation, I had plenty of time to reflect on my military career. I was well aware it would soon be over. I thought about everything I had seen and done, the thanks I had received over time and the awards I had earned. I knew the Army could keep me shadow posted for a few months so I could complete my 20 years' service which had always been my goal. However, mentally I just could not function properly and a lot of decisions were made for me by other people. The worst decision was not to take the Medical Corps' offer of looking after me until I had completed two decades' service. I had always intended to do a minimum of 20 years' service. It was important to me personally (my father had served 20 and I wanted to get the gold bar on my long service medal just like him) and financially, because whenever I left I automatically received a generous pension. I did not know much about medical pensions but I knew they could be stopped at any time. I was so disappointed and saddened by having to leave before achieving my goal. I wrote to the Governor General to request that my case be looked at and consideration be given to awarding me the bar for my Defence Long Service Medal. I was not actually leaving the Army, I was being medically discharged. I never got a response to my letter.

When talking to the nurses and Malcolm about my time in the Army, I spoke of my doubts about my achievements. Malcolm suggested that I write down everything I could remember doing so that I had some positives to focus on. Three days later I read over my list and was surprised. During my career I had been on 31 postings and detachments, serving as a medic in seven different corps. I was an instructor on 21 courses ranging from first aid to military skills. I had provided level one medical support to 90 different activities and supported numerous field exercises and live fire range practices. I had attended 19 military courses and 17 civilian courses and never failed any of them. I was awarded the Military Skills Award, the Land Commander's Commendation and the C.F. Marks award which is given by the medical corps to one soldier each year for outstanding work and contributions to the corps. I received that award while working in the RAP at 8/9RAR. I had served overseas three times, including with the UN. I was also a qualified Justice of the Peace and a St John's Ambulance instructor.

There was no time when I had not enjoyed being a medic in the Army. I always tried to do my best, although I am sure there were times when there was room for improvement. I particularly enjoyed being able to pass on my own knowledge to other up-and-coming medical and nursing staff. I always tried to maintain a positive attitude in all areas of the Army and my life and always tried to lead by example. I would never ask anyone to do something I did not think I was capable of doing myself. I only hoped I did not get it wrong too often. I believe I was a well-respected staff sergeant medical assistant. There was no course I would not do and I went out of my way to do as many as I could. I wanted to have a full understanding of each unit I was posted to and what the soldiers in those units had to go through. Every unit has a different role and tasks within the Army. From a medical planning point of view, I needed to know what was being described to me over a radio so I could make the correct judgment, knowing the type of injuries a soldier could be suffering and how to extract them. From an evacuation point of view, I had to know what was available to me, whether it was stretcher-bearers or helicopters, and then be able to call on them and know how best to use them. During my career in the Royal Australian Army Medical Corps, and the Army in general, I believe I did all right. I respected each and every soldier I met and trusted their ability. I loved Army life and wanted to continue my service until the compulsory retirement age of 55, hopefully gaining the promotion necessary to become the RSM of the Medical Corps.

But now none of this was going to happen, which was terribly disappointing. I was going to be discharged, medically unfit for service due to PTSD, the result of my service in Rwanda and at Kibeho. There was no farewell for me when I left the Army. My life had changed drastically and somehow I was going to have to learn to live with my mental illness. On 1st July, 1997 I was medically discharged after serving in the medical corps for 19 years and 74 days. I was just nine months short of my 20-year goal. I was devastated.

Chapter Twelve

Starting over

"The nightmares were so bad I was too scared to go to sleep, so I would drink until I was close to passing out. I got careless with my medication and would forget to take it so I started feeling even worse. I put on weight despite hardly eating. I hated going anywhere except to the local pub."

Being discharged felt like losing a life-long friend. I was going to miss the Army terribly but I also knew it had to be that way. I still could not function mentally the way I needed to. I was plagued by fits of depression and the nightmares and flashbacks still haunted me. When I went to the bank I sometimes had a bad panic attack, because I had an irrational fear it might be robbed and I did not know what I would do to stop it. I would lose my car in the car park, forcing me to walk home and return at night when the car park was empty so I could find it. I could not concentrate long enough to read a book. I felt extremely unsafe in crowds which made it very challenging to go out. This was not the way I wanted to live and it was not long before I was back at New Farm clinic. I was scared.

I spent the next month trying to learn how to live with PTSD. Being told I could not talk to the people around me about my experiences in Rwanda and Kibeho was starting to grate. I was allowed talk to the nurses but they did not really seem to care. I realise now they were there to listen to me but not necessarily to answer all my questions. All I could tell my fellow patients was that I had been a soldier and I had PTSD. I took up smoking again.

The second time I was discharged from the clinic I felt a little better. Malcolm had made some adjustments to my medication and I had learned ways to cope with my condition. I started seeing a counsellor but that did not last long. He did not believe what I said I had witnessed in Kibeho. He thought I was making up a lot of the stories to make things appear worse than they actually where. He had never even heard of the place. Another problem I faced was no longer having the medical and moral support a soldier normally gets from the Army. There was no one to talk to. Everyone I had served with in Rwanda was either serving interstate or had been discharged.

By now I was on a totally and permanently incapacitated (TPI) pension from Veteran Affairs and a Class A medical pension from the Defence Force. A small amount of compensation from the Defence Force was enough for a deposit on a house. I bought a house not far from Kelsey and Alanna so I could see them regularly. I also bought a small car. I thought I was set, but before long depression set in again. I ignored the symptoms and instead began consuming vast amounts of alcohol as a way of making myself feel better. The nightmares and flashbacks were still bothering me and I had started to feel weighed down by a terrible guilt about Kibeho. Had I done enough? Could I have done better? Could I have saved just one more baby from that room full of children? Day and night these questions ran through my head.

Drinking helped numb the bad feelings. I had looked on at Kibeho with a loaded weapon. But under orders I had not used it to save men, women and children from being slaughtered. Images flashed into my head without warning, triggered by everyday smells and sounds. They would make me panic, and I would be convinced that something terrible was about to happen. The nightmares were so bad I was too scared to go to sleep, so I would drink until I was close to passing out. I got careless with my medication and would forget to take it so I started feeling even worse. I put on weight despite hardly eating. I hated going anywhere except to the local pub. It was inevitable that I would be done for drink driving.

I went back to New Farm clinic to try and sort myself out. This time I had to admit to Dr Malcolm Foxcroft that I had an alcohol problem. I spent the next month learning how to deal with my nightmares. Each time I had one the sisters would make me get up, check the time and then sit quietly until my heart rate settled down again. I gradually came to accept that the nightmares were going to be part of my life and I would have to learn to live with them instead of trying to fight them. The nurses helped reinforce to me that dreams could not hurt me physically and by following just a few basic rules I could go back to sleep more easily. They helped me understand that alcohol was not the answer and taking my medication properly was. Malcolm got me to write down the nightmares in a diary so I could better explain to him what I was dreaming about. I have reproduced two extracts from my diary here. The first one concerns a nightmare that happened four months after I returned to Australia, a year before I diagnosed with PTSD.

"I am working in the resuscitation room when a patient who has been injured comes in. I start to work on him when it becomes apparent that it is a child. The child, we believe, is going to die. As we are working, we stop to see what is happening. The child gradually starts to vanish before my eyes, with the meat of the legs beginning to dissolve. I am absolutely amazed that the child is still alive. I work some more on resuscitating the child as it continues to disintegrate. We are all waiting and wishing for this child to die, but it will not. We are getting more and more impatient as it continues to disappear until finally it just consists of a head, ribs and a tiny set of lungs. I am amazed and disgusted that this thing dares to still be alive when I know that it would be better off dead. Then the face I see on this child is the face of my seven-year-old daughter."

I woke from that dream soaked in sweat and in a complete state of panic. I couldn't go back to sleep for the rest of the night and watched TV until daylight.

This was fairly typical of the nightmares I was having at the time. It made no sense at all; it was just a reminder of some of the horrendous things that happened at Kibeho. There were so many casualties, many worse than you could imagine, and yet they were still walking and talking. We treated them knowing full well their chances of survival were slim to none. In some cases we believed death would have been easier for them. I believe in my dreams my mind was trying to clear some of the distress I continued to feel. I was trying to make sense of it all and failing.

This second extract was written after I spent some time in hospital learning how to deal with my demons, using a combination of cognitive behavioural therapy I learnt in group sessions and medication. Within 20 minutes of waking up I was able to deal with my distress and get back to sleep.

"I am loading patients into a helicopter. They have to climb a rope to get to it. The helicopter is in the air above me and cannot land. The doctor with me had to go somewhere else so I am loading the patients myself. There are seven patients but two of them are pregnant women, so to me this makes a total of nine. I am about to get them on board but they will not throw the rope down for me to climb. The helicopter turns sideways and I am amazed that it is going to leave without me. It is still above me when it rises out of control and smashes into the moon and explodes. I am required to go forward and count the bodies which are now skeletons sunk into solid rock. I take a photographer with me who is meant to photograph the bodies but he is really upset. I tell him to get on with his job because I don't want to have to take photos as well as do my job. I go around this mass of red rock and count all the embedded skeletons and include the two child skeletons to total nine. I then report to the doctor I am working with for my debrief and she tells me that I have done OK, but I should not have let two pregnant women on the aircraft. She said this in a matter-of-fact way as if it was no big deal. And then she said 'Just don't let it happen again'."

I think dreams like his were my subconscious trying to sort out if I had done the right thing in Kibeho. There was always some sort of authoritarian figure in the dreams who debriefed me about how I had performed in the situation. Some of the figures would forgive me for making mistakes. Others suggested better ways of handling the situation. Perhaps my mind was trying to find a kind of peace through the advice and forgiveness of an imaginary third person.

While I was in hospital I began going to Alcoholics Anonymous a couple of times a week. Four weeks after going into hospital I was finally discharged. I appeared in court to face the consequences of my drink driving charge and left with a $1,000 fine and no licence for a year. At least I was getting better at dealing with the nightmares and I was doing it without the large amount of alcohol I had consumed during the previous two years.

It was about this time that Malcolm decided we should try eye movement desenitisation and reprocessing (EMDR) to see if it would help with my flashbacks. EMDR can be used in conjunction with cognitive behavioural therapy and psychiatric therapy to help with cases of PTSD, but it does not work for everyone. At the time it was a little experimental. Each Saturday morning while I was in hospital I used this technique to visualise and then focus on a particular scene from Kibeho. Then I worked on it until it "disappeared" from my mind. Somehow this way of moving my eyes back and forth horizontally helped my brain to reprogram the way I saw things. I could tell when it worked because I would get a sudden jolt like an electric shock. When it did not work I felt nothing. I can now visualise the scenes we worked on successfully with little or no discomfort at all. Each trip into New Farm clinic gave me a little more knowledge about how to cope with living with PTSD.

That's not to say there were not setbacks. There always are with PTSD as with everything in life. I have good days and bad days. Some days can still turn upside down as the result of some very little thing. One Anzac Day, a couple of years after being discharged, I went to my local RSL for the dawn service. I was really looking forward to the day because it was going to be the first time I had chosen to wear my medals to the RSL. A Vietnam veteran, who I thought was a good friend of mine, commented on how good my plastic medals were. In essence he was saying his were real and mine were worthless because they were UN medals. I was bitterly disappointed in him for saying this because he had no idea. He had worked in the quartermaster store during his Vietnam service! I felt sick for the rest of the day and got on the grog for a few weeks after that.

September 11, 2001 was a really big setback for me because my belief that everything was safe in the western world was shown to be very naïve.

The fact that the World Trade Centre towers were destroyed by terrorists in the supposedly most secure country in the world completely shattered my beliefs. *What is the point of it all, I thought*. And then I got on the grog again. If I went out I would get the doomsday feeling all over again, so I tried to stay home as much as possible. I bought cartons and cartons of beer and drank myself into peaceful oblivion. I went back into hospital and this time spent Christmas and New Year there. I was lucky enough to meet a couple of Vietnam veterans who also suffered PTSD, who told me their stories and their troubles when they returned to Australia. At least I did not have red paint thrown at me as I marched down the main street of Townsville after returning from Vietnam. I was also relieved that I could talk to them about my experiences and have them understand how I felt. It certainly made me feel a little better knowing that I was not alone.

One veteran I got to know very well was Gary Shepherd, or Shep for short. I visited him at his place in the country and it was the best time I'd had since leaving the Army. He lived in a caravan with a lean-to. He used a generator to charge up batteries for a fridge and cooked on an open fire. Talking to him was probably the best therapy for me, because neither of us made judgments about the other or about what we said. We could describe the most horrific things and still have a good laugh. I went there many times. I was shattered when his son rang one day to tell me Shep had passed away during the night. I spiralled into the depths of depression again.

There were times when all seemed to be going well so I stopped taking my medication, thinking that I did not need it anymore. The problem was after stopping the drugs I began to drink in the local pub and the whole cycle began again. I lost my licence again for drink driving and found myself back in hospital. It was also getting expensive. I had written off two cars worth about $40,000 and I was still paying them off. My relationship with Kelsey and Alanna was almost non-existent. Sometimes I was too drunk to attend their birthday parties. During those periods the only thing I seemed to have any interest in was where the next beer was coming from.

Strangely, feeling good could also send me into a depression. One day I received a message from a woman called Sally Stone asking me to ring her. She was seeking information about Kibeho and the soldiers who had been there. Sally worked on the Channel Nine television programme *Sixty Minutes* and wanted to interview some of the soldiers who were at Kibeho. I was excited by this, because *I thought* that finally the public would understand that peacekeeping operations are not the great tax-free holiday that some people made them out to be. Another plus was that through Sally I was able to get in contact with Nico again. Unfortunately the extreme high I felt had a bad effect on me and I ended up back in hospital. The high turned into disappointment and deep depression as Sally and I came up against brick walls trying to get information from some people still serving in the Army. One soldier was advised by someone in authority that anyone still serving would face immediate discharge if they spoke to the media about Kibeho and the Australian involvement. Nico and I struggled to find someone Sally could talk to until I remembered that Jordo was now out of the army and working in a security business in New Guinea. Even with all of Sally's hard work it took four years until Channel 9 actually broadcast the story on the *Sunday* show. In all that time it seemed to me that nobody was interested. The Army said nothing and some of the soldiers who served in Kibeho either were not allowed to say anything or simply refused to.

One of the most stressful times for me is when the Defence Force section that pays my pension decides it is time to review whether I warrant remaining on the Class A medical pension. This review happens about every two years. I usually have to go into Brisbane to see one of their nominated psychiatrists for a review, which unfortunately involves having to describe what my time in Kibeho was like. I have to describe it all in detail every time I am reviewed. I also have to go through all my own signs and symptoms and list the treatments I am having, the medication I am on and the time I have spent in hospital. By the time I leave I am usually quite ill. I have twice thrown up in the street on the way home. It usually takes a couple of weeks to recover. Now I take a lot of medication before I go.

One of the difficulties is people cannot see a mental illness whereas they can a physical disability. In my darker moments I have told Malcolm that I would rather have lost both my legs than part of my mind because at least then people would be able to see my injuries. His response was that most people who suffer PTSD have similar opinions. It's no wonder some of the extremely desperate patients end up committing suicide.

After a stay in hospital when I had to start my medication all over again I gave Alcoholics Anonymous another go. In the end I came to realise that all the decisions made about me were really up to me. I was the only one who could help me. Sure, the doctors, nurses, counsellors, friends and AA could give me great advice but I had to choose what I wanted to do. It was up to me to take charge. I needed to get PTSD under my command and not the other way around. As soon as I recognised – and took – the right steps there was a great improvement in a lot of areas of my life. I started running again and went on a diet, gradually losing the 20 kilograms I had stacked on since my discharge. During the next six months I got reasonably fit and started learning Tae Kwon Do. At last I was starting to get some control over my own life.

Tae Kwon Do has become an important way to help control my PTSD. I started learning it as a way to fill in my time, but as I slowly progressed I found it to be a great way to gain a better feeling of self control. Tae Kwon Do helps join my mind, body and spirit together as one. Instead of feeling that my mind and body are two separate things I now use the power of my mind to control my body to do things I thought it could not do. My instructor, Lenny Too (third Dan), knows about the PTSD and he lets me progress at my own pace, because there are times when something that would normally 10 minutes to learn takes me weeks. He is the most patient instructor I have ever had. The philosophical side of Tae Kwon Do has also helped give me some peace of mind. My master instructor Trevor Dicks, a sixth Dan international instructor and the grading master, gives lessons on this subject. It has been really good for the whole of me.

All of this has been a way of regaining some control over my life. I have learnt how to live and cope with nightmares and flashbacks using behavioural therapy as well as medication when I need it. My need to consume vast amounts of alcohol seems to have passed and I feel a whole lot better about myself. My self-esteem has improved since I shed the extra weight and got some of my fitness back. Overall, things are looking up. For the first time in a very long time I am starting to feel happy again. It has taken nine years to get to this point, a point where I feel I am in a reasonable state of mind.

Chapter Thirteen

Life goes on

"*I cannot escape the nightmares and occasional flashback but I have learnt how to deal with these as they occur. I can usually read my own signs and symptoms and adjust my medication or my life to cope. There will be times when I do not read them that well and that is where Nicky comes in. With her help, I am moving forward again.*"

It's 2008 and the last time I was in New Farm clinic was a little over two and a half years ago. I think that has a lot to do with the fact that when I was there last I met another patient called Nicole. As soon as we met we both felt a kind of special bond, even though she is a lot younger than me. When I left hospital I moved back to Brisbane from the farm where I was living. Having lost my licence for a second time (this time for 14 months), I wanted to be closer to Kelsey and Alanna, but I also hoped that perhaps Nicky would move in with me. At first we had a bit of a hard time from some people because of our age difference and the fact we both suffered a form of mental illness. But we struggled on together.

A couple of months after moving back to Brisbane, my friend Nico rang to tell me that Channel Nine was looking for me to do an interview for the *Sunday* programme. They were doing a cover story about the soldiers who had served in Rwanda, particularly Kibeho. The interview was arranged, with Ross Coulthart asking the questions and Christopher Zinn the producer. During the interview I was given a box of my diaries and photos that I had not seen since I gave it to Sally Stone a few years before. When I opened the box to explain to Kelsey what the photos were about I was hit by some terrible flashbacks. I thought I was nearly over them but I became quite ill and had to stop the interview. Ross came down the backyard with me and helped settle me down. I tried to place my mind on automatic and continued with the interview. Christopher Zinn rang me a week before the airing which gave me time to prepare myself. I even took some medication before watching. Just in case. When the show finally went to air, I was ready.

To my relief, the programme was a great success. It accurately depicted everything we had been trying to tell people about Kibeho and did it in a respectful way. Even people I knew quite well were astounded that it occurred and that Australian soldiers had been there. Many people did not even know Australia had sent troops to Rwanda. At last the old myth of peacekeeping service with the UN being just a bit of a holiday and a good way of earning extra money was put away for good.

There was a bonus to come out of show which none of us expected. The whole Australian mission was finally upgraded from non-warlike service to war-like service. This meant that we were now entitled to a service pension which would certainly help financially. We would also be entitled to wear the Australian Active Service Medal rather than just the Australian Service Medal. This was a little piece of a compensation for the horrors we had seen and that some of us continued to suffer. It had taken more than 10 years for the government to upgrade our service. The day I read that news on the internet I had tears in my eyes. Finally we had been given some meagre recognition.

A few of the comments on the *Sunday* programme really hit home for me. Jordo said that if he had killed one of the RPA soldiers, or even just fired his weapon, we probably would all be dead. I have no doubt that this is absolutely true. In fact, I am sure that at one stage we were going to be killed because how could the RPA allow us to live after witnessing the mass murder of unarmed, helpless and starving men, women and children? Why we were not killed I do not know. Ross Coulthart said that the figure of 4,000 slaughtered was a gross underestimate. This I believe because when Jordo and the CSM did their body count they got to 4,500 before being forced to stop. A CNN reporter at the time suggested that as many as 25,000 may have been killed. The RPA removed a lot of the dead during the night and buried them in mass graves. Justin Fiddler said that, as a soldier, you can sometimes find it hard to admit dealing with the trauma is mentally stressful and Robbie Lucas agreed. Nico said the same thing and I agree with them. I am aware that there have been soldiers who have played on PTSD to get pensions, but there are also really sick people who do not play on it and struggle to remain on a pension. It is unfair that they always have to justify themselves to others. Jordo is well. He has dealt with it and continues to work. It was the same for Churchy, but they were both from the Special Air Service Regiment and may have been better trained to handle situations like that.

The question of why some people or soldiers suffer PTSD and others do not is intriguing. There is no answer. I knew a soldier who served in Vietnam and never had any problems at all until he came across a vehicle accident while on a peacekeeping mission in Cambodia about 20 years later and suffered horrific flashbacks. I met an 89-year-old man in the clinic who had been a prisoner of the Japanese during WWII and was forced to work on the Burma railway. He had not suffered any lasting mental issues for more than 50 years after his service. He had been having nightmares for a couple of weeks and felt terribly depressed so was admitted to New Farm clinic where he was diagnosed with PTSD. PTSD can strike at any time and can affect anyone.

Not long after the *Sunday* programme, Nico and his family came to Queensland and we met up on the Gold Coast. I was scared and nervous about seeing him again but we quickly got over that and had a terrific time swapping stories about Rwanda and Kibeho over quite a few beers.

I continue to struggle with some memories. Earlier this year I had the sudden realisation that grabbing several small babies by the scruff of the shirt in one hand so that I could get them to safety was not really a normal thing to do. The situation I had been in at Kibeho when that happened was unbelievable and not normal. I struggled with this thought for several days until it started to fade from my mind. What I had learned in New Farm clinic enabled me to deal with this episode in a reasonably rational way. Had it been a couple of years earlier I would have fallen apart and probably ended up in hospital again after a drinking session. Nico and I have remained friends and talk on the phone every few weeks. He even came up to Brisbane to be at my wedding, when Nicky and I took the plunge. Nicky and I have a very special relationship. We understand each other completely. You won't find anything like it in a novel or see it in a movie. It is beautiful. We try to support each other both mentally and physically. Of course it is hard work for us with our mental illnesses especially when little Bella was first born, but it is all worth it. We both knew we were meant to be together despite what other people said, so we decided to get married just to show them all we were for real.

Nicky and I have since moved a little further out of Brisbane into another rented house. I got my licence back and vowed never to drink and drive again. Not even after one beer. I occasionally struggle with PTSD, but I cope better. Sometimes it will sneak up on me. The smell of the rubbish dump reminds me of Kibeho and sometimes seeing raw meat in the butcher's shop can transport me straight back to the injured people I treated. I have times, particularly on Anzac Day, when my left hand shakes uncontrollably just like when I was doing the resus on the small girl in the hospital. There is nothing I can do except wait for it to settle down. A couple of times I have been invited to speak to Kelsey's class about my experiences and medals. On each occasion I have nearly broken down in tears. But all of these things are quite normal for me and will be part of my life until the day I die.

There are some questions that people always ask.

How do I explain to the ordinary person what it was like in Kibeho?

I start by asking them, "Have you ever seen anyone die?" Some say, "Yes, a relative or a friend". I ask them how they felt about that. Then I ask them, "Have you ever seen anyone murdered?" Hardly anyone has. Then I ask them, "What do you think it would feel like to watch 8,000 helpless men, women and children being murdered while you are holding a fully loaded rifle? You have to just sit there and watch then spend the next day trying to pick the right people to save and treat." I ask them, "How do you think you would feel about that?" Nobody has ever been able to answer that question.

Did I ever try to work again?

Yes, I did. I started doing volunteer work to see if I could handle it, but I fell to pieces and had to stop. I tried to be a volunteer for St John's Ambulance only to be told that my Army medical qualifications meant nothing and I would have to attend the basic first aid course. To me that was a joke, because I had 20 years of experience as an Army medic and had previously been a St John's Ambulance instructor. I tried to work as an enrolled nurse and applied to a number of hospitals, but nobody would recognise my Army service. St John's gave no particular reason as to why I would have to start at the basic level, but the hospitals advised me that I could not be recognised as an enrolled nurse because I had been out of the Army more than two years. I tried mowing lawns and handyman work, but I found it impossible to communicate with people to organise jobs.

Have I tried to do further education?

Yes, I have. In 2003 I enrolled at the Australian College of Natural Medicine, doing only three subjects a semester. The college would not recognise any of my Army qualifications, so I had to start the course with anatomy and physiology as one of the subjects. I used to teach this on Army medical courses so studying it all over again seemed pointless. After a while I started to stress about my subjects. Eventually it all got too much for me and I had to withdraw. I simply could not absorb what they were trying to impart. My powers of concentration were very poor, so poor in fact that I had difficulty remembering what had been said at the beginning of the lesson when we got to the end. This was another symptom of PTSD and I was getting really frustrated and angry. After that I was admitted into New Farm clinic again for three weeks.

Do I still have nightmares or flashbacks?

At least twice a week I have nightmares which wake me up. I usually have to get out of my sweaty bed and leave the room so I can settle myself down using the techniques I was taught in hospital. Once in a while I use medication. I get the occasional flashback but try and remove myself from anything that might cause them. I don't go to the butcher or the dump on a hot day. Any television programme portraying dead children is hard to watch. A car backfiring can make me duck for cover. Fireworks remind me of machinegun fire.

Am I still on medication?

I will probably be on antidepressants for the rest of my life. I have other medication that slows me down if I cannot settle after flashbacks or nightmares. I often have to take sleeping tablets at night. All the medication is self-administered but very closely monitored by my local doctor and a psychiatrist. I tried several times to stop taking the medication and within a week or two started falling apart.

Do I still see a psychiatrist?

I usually see him once a fortnight for a chat and for some EMDR whenever I need it. He monitors my medication and will admit me into New Farm clinic if either of us thinks I need it. Sometimes when life gets too much I will be admitted to hospital for a rest and treatment. In fact as this book was going to print I needed to spend two weeks back in New Farm clinic for some rest and for what I like to call "top up" treatment. My psychiatrist will only admit me into the hospital where he works so he can see me each day.

Do I still have a problem with alcohol?

I believe I do not, which admittedly is one of the tricks of being an alcoholic. I just have to be very careful if I do drink. I won't drink any more than six stubbies of beer or a couple of glasses of wine at one time. I rarely go to pubs or clubs. I am very aware that it would be easy to give in to alcohol and use it as a crutch again. It is a struggle but I do not want to live the life of an alcoholic. I never drink and drive. However I do still smoke cigarettes.

Does anything annoy you about your service in Rwanda?

Yes. For me, looking on the internet and finding a whole website dedicated to someone who claims to have had the hardest time in Rwanda, particularly at Kibeho, really gets me going. Yes, most of the people who claim to have been at Kibeho were actually there, but not until after the massacre. There are people who will claim to have been there but never actually left the hospital. They are just trying to big note themselves, unfortunately at a cost to those of us who were there. It was a complete shock to me to see some of these sites when we were advised not to talk too much about our service there.

Do you hold a grudge against the Army or Defence Force?

No, I don't. Some people who have been discharged feel they have been hard

done by. I feel I was discharged for being no longer fit enough to serve in the Army. I know the Defence Force tries its best to look after people who have suffered injuries or illnesses, particularly if it happened on overseas service. But it cannot afford to hold on to anyone who is not able to do their job. To function to the best of its ability the Defence Force must have fit people.

Do you think you received enough recognition for your service in Rwanda, particularly Kibeho?

No, I don't. I believe that each and every one of the 32 soldiers who were in Kibeho from April 18th to 22nd in 1995 should have received some sort of special recognition. Four soldiers received the Gallantry Medal. A few others received minor medals and commendations. I believe those who were there should have been recognised with a unit citation or unit bravery award. As Ross Coulthart said in the *Sunday* programme, the Australians showed incredible restraint. So many acts of bravery, for example Jordo's retrieval of the boy under fire, went unrecognised. George Gittoes, the war artist, said that Australians had not come under as much intense and continuous fire since World War II. Nearly everyone at Kibeho remembers rounds landing around them or whizzing by them, but they still carried on with their tasks. It took more than 10 years just for our service to be recognised as war-like instead of a non-hazardous peacekeeping duty. Vietnam veterans at least had an identifiable enemy to shoot at and were allowed to do so. We had neither of those options. It was, as Paul Copeland, the national president of the Australian Peacekeepers and Peacemakers Association, said: we were sent into a war zone with weapons, but with our hands tied behind our backs.

What is the message you are trying to get across by writing this book?

I want people to know that UN peacekeeping operations are not necessarily peaceful. They can be as dangerous as any recognised conflict like WWII, Vietnam, Iraq or Afghanistan. The restraints placed on our defence personnel today are totally different to 30 years ago. Warfare has changed. The media can now beam army actions into the lounge rooms of viewers a world away as it happens. For me, it is time to give a first-hand account of a little-known moment in Australian military history.

How does PTSD affect your everyday life?

I have an extremely short temper and tend to fly off the handle a bit. I need to know everything that is happening around me all the time. When I need to do something I want it out of the way immediately whether it's done properly or not. I am not all that keen on going out of the house. It's a struggle, but I do it. I have very little patience for people who are sick or injured, because I cannot help comparing them with the sick or injured in Rwanda. I rarely sleep a whole night. It's more like four or five hours of broken sleep, often less. Sometimes I will sleep all day. I can't watch a war movie. Night sweats mean that even in winter I sleep in my underpants under a light blanket. So many things have changed in my life but that's just the way I am now.

How is life for you now?

Life is good. Nicky and I live with our 16-month-old daughter, Bella Rose, in the outer northern suburbs of Brisbane. We live simply, generally on a day-to-day basis, but we do plan for the future. Kelsey visits occasionally and stays for a few days during the school holidays. Alanna is studying at university and rings now and then. Nico and I keep in touch. My brother Ken lives on a farm near Toowoomba and often visits. I ring my dad every couple of weeks. Sadly, my mother passed away early this year. I don't miss being a soldier as much as when I was initially discharged. But I do miss the mateship. I have bumped into a couple of the people who served in Rwanda, and only one person who was in Kibeho with me. I really miss riding in helicopters and going out bush, but I would not trade any of it for my life with Nicky.

I maintain a reasonable level of fitness by running and practicing Tae Kwon Do. I do not run every day and I do not run competitively anymore, only for fun and fitness. I have progressed to brown belt in Tae Kwon Do. One day I hope to achieve the black belt although I do find that grading is quite nerve-racking. I like to walk. Sometimes I go for a bushwalk because I miss being out in the field.

I am aware that I now live with fairly severe PTSD and that I always will. I am fine with that. I have met enough people with disabilities or mental illness to know that enjoying life is always possible if you live with the condition rather than in a state of denial. If I need to go to hospital again then so be it. I cannot escape the nightmares and occasional flashbacks but I have learnt how to deal with them as they occur. I can usually read my own signs and symptoms and adjust my medication or my life to cope. There will be times when I do not read them that well and that is where Nicky comes in. With her help, I am moving forward again.

Life will go on.

Terry
Pickard

Terry Pickard was born in Sydney in 1959. He left school in 1976 in grade ten, and after drifting for a couple of years decided to follow in his father's footsteps and become a career soldier. He enlisted into the Army in 1978. Not wanting to inflict harm as a fighting soldier, he joined the Medical Corps so he could assist others instead.

Terry completed his medical orderly course and his postings include: 1st Australian Field Hospital, Ingleburn; Proof and Experimental Establishment, Port Wakefield, SA (Artillery); School Of Army Health, Healesville; Headquarters 1st Military District, Brisbane; 1st Military Hospital, Yeronga, Queensland; 8th/9th Battalion Royal Australian Regiment; School Of Artillery, Manly, New South Wales; and 2nd/14th Light Horse Regiment, Enoggera Queensland (Armoured Corps). Overseas postings and tours include: Australian Rifle Company, Butterworth, Malaysia, Rifle Company, Brunei and on operations in 1995 to Rwanda as part of the United Nations Assistance Mission Rwanda (UNAMIR), where in April 1995 he witnessed the Kibeho Massacre. Terry was promoted to staff sergeant in December 1995. He was diagnosed with severe post-traumatic stress disorder in 1997 as a result of the events in Rwanda and was medically discharged in July 1997 – nine months short of his 20 years' service.

Terry's awards include: Military Skills Award 1988 for excellence in first aid instructing DFSM 1993; 15 years' service; ASM Clasp Rwanda 1995; UN Medal with UNAMIR Ribbon 1995; ANZAC Peace Prize 1995 as a member of the Australian contingent to Rwanda; Land Commander Commendation 1996 for outstanding service in Kibeho; C.F. Marks Award 1996 for outstanding service with Medical Corps; ASM Clasp S.E. Asia 1998 for service in Malaysia in 1988; and AASM clasp Rwanda 2006, updating the ASM Clasp Rwanda.

Terry is married to Nicole and lives in Brisbane. He has three daughters, Bella Rose, Kelsey, Alanna and a son Daniel.

Glossary

Military terms and abbreviations

.30 cal MG:	30 caliber machinegun
.50 cal MG:	50 caliber machinegun
2IC:	Second-in-command of a section (lance corporal), platoon, (sergeant) company, (captain), battalion (major)
AASM:	Australian Active Service Medal
ADF:	Australian Defence Force
AK 47:	Russian\Chinese 7.62 mm automatic assault rifle used by RPA
AKM:	Updated AK47 automatic assault rifle used by RPA
AMB:	Ambulance
AME:	Air medical evacuation
Ammo:	Ammunition
AMSF:	Australian Medical Support Force
ANZAC:	Australian and New Zealand Army Corps
AO:	Area of Operations
APC:	Armored personnel carrier
ARA:	Australian Regular Army
AS MSF HQ:	Australian service medical support force headquarters
ASC:	Australian Service Contingent
ASM:	Australian Service Medal
AUSMED:	Australian medical facility (hospital in Kigali)
AWOL:	Absent without leave
BET:	Battle efficiency test
BFA:	Basic Fitness Assessment
Boozer:	Bar
Brew:	Cup of coffee or tea
BRIG:	Brigadier
BRL:	Battalion recreation leave
Bug out:	To escape
CAPT:	Captain
CARE Australia:	CARE Australia
Casevac:	Casualty evacuation
Cav:	Abbreviation for cavalry or light armoured units
CCP:	Casualty collection point
CDF Commendation:	Chief of the Defence Force Commendation

CGS Commendation:	Chief of the General Staff Commendation
CHK:	Central hospital, Kigali
Chopper:	Helicopter
CHQ:	Company headquarters
Civvy:	Civilian
Claymore:	Portable, above ground, directional, command detonated mine, loaded with 700 ball bearings
Click:	Slang for kilometer
CO:	Commanding Officer (Lieutenant Colonel)
COL:	Colonel
Comms:	Communications
Coy:	Company (consisting of 90–120 men)
CP:	Command post
CPL:	Corporal (a section commander)
CQ:	Company quartermaster
CQMS:	Company Quartermaster Sergeant, a staff sergeant
CRP:	Combat ration pack
CSC:	Conspicuous Service Cross
CSM:	Company Sergeant Major, a warrant officer class two
CSM:	Conspicuous Service Medal
Digger:	Nickname for Australian soldier
Doxy:	Anti-malaria tablet taken three times a day
DP:	Displaced persons
Dustoff:	Acronym for a helicopter for casualty evacuation
EHS:	Emergency health services
ETHIOBATT:	Ethiopian Battalion
F88 Steyr:	5.56 mm individual weapon
F89 LSW Minimi:	5.56 mm Light Support Weapon
Flak Jacket:	A vest worn over the uniform to stop bomb secondary fragmentation
FFR:	Fresh field rations
Fragged:	Injured or killed by fragmentation from artillery, mortars or grenade
F-RGF:	Former-Rwandese government forces
GANBATT:	Ghana Battalion
GPMG:	General purpose machinegun

Grunt:	An infantryman
HE:	High explosive ordnance
Helo:	Helicopter
Hexy or Hexamine:	Solid fuel blocks for heating food and water
Hootch, hootchie:	Nickname for personal shelter or lodgings
HQ:	Headquarters
Huey:	Bell helicopter
IA:	Immediate action
ICRV:	International Committee of Red Cross
ICV:	Immune Complex-based Vaccine
ICU:	Intensive care unit
ID:	Identification
IDP:	Internally displaced person
INDBATT:	Indian Battalion
In Country:	In Rwanda
INT:	Intelligence
INTOFF:	Intelligence Officer
IV:	Intravenous
JNCO:	Junior Non-commissioned Officer
KIA:	Killed in action
Kiwi:	Nickname for New Zealanders
LCPL or (Lance Jack):	Lance Corporal (second-in-command of a section of nine men)
LHQ:	Land Headquarters
LP:	Landing place for one helicopter
LT COL:	Lieutenant Colonel
LT:	Lieutenant (a platoon commander)
LZ:	Landing zone for several helicopters
M16:	5.56 mm US automatic rifle
MAINTDEM:	Maintenance Demand. A resupply of rations, ammo and equipment. Usually by helicopter
MAJ:	Major (a company commander)
MALICOY:	Mali Company
MAWIBATT:	Mawi Battalion
MED:	Medical
Mess:	Dining area for soldiers e.g. Officers' Mess, Sergeants' Mess, Other Ranks' Mess

MFO:	Mortar Fire Officer
MG:	Medal of Gallantry
MG:	Machinegun
MP:	Military Police
MSF:	Medecins Sans Frontieres (Doctors without borders)
MSR:	Main supply route
Muzzunga:	Rwandan slang for white man
Negligent Discharge (ND):	Unintentional firing of a weapon
Net:	Radio network
NCO:	Non-commissioned Officer
NGO:	Non-government Organisation
NIBATT:	Nigerian Battalion
NLT:	No later than
NSC:	Nursing Service Cross
OC:	Officer Commanding
O (orders) -Group: by the commander	A meeting at which a unit's officers or equivalent are briefed
OHP:	Overhead preotection
OIC:	Officer in Command
OJT:	On-the-job training
OPDEM:	Operational demand
OP RETOUR:	Operation RETOUR (designed to return Rwandese displaced people to their communes)
OP SPT:	Operational support unit
OP TAMAR:	Operation TAMAR (Troops and Medical Aid Rwanda designed to spt UN troops medically)
OP TURQUOISE:	Operation TURQUOISE (area in SW of Rwanda as a safe haven designed to protect Rwandese displaced people)
OP:	Observation post
OPS:	Operations
OPSO:	Operations Officer
OR:	Other ranks
ORBAT:	Order of battle
PHQ:	Platoon headquarters
Picket:	Duty, radio, sentry or telephone picket
PL COMD:	Platoon Commander

PL SGT:	Platoon Sergeant (second-in-command of a platoon)
PL:	Platoon (consisting of 30 men)
PR:	Public relations
PT:	Physical training
PTE:	Private soldier
PTI:	Physical training instructor
PTSD:	Post Traumatic Stress Disorder
Q-Store:	Quartermaster's store
QM:	Quartermaster
QRF:	Quick Reaction Force
R&R:	Rest and relaxation (usually taken in Nairobi, Kenya for a few days)
RAAF:	Royal Australian Air Force
RAAMC:	Royal Australian Army Medical Corps
RAInf:	Royal Australian Infantry
RAP:	Regimental aid post
RAR:	Royal Australian Regiment (Infantry)
Recce:	Reconnaisance
RGF:	Rwandese Government Forces
Route Clearance:	Authorisation to go through on a route through another unit's TAOR or AO
RPA:	Rwandese Patriotic Army
RPF:	Rwandese Patriotic Front
RPG:	Rocket propelled grenade
RQMS:	Regimental Quartermaster Sergeant same rank as RSM
RSL:	Returned Services League of Australia
RSM:	Regimental Sergeant Major
RSM-A:	Regimental Sergeant Major – Army
RTA:	Return to Australia
RTU:	Return to unit
S & S:	Signs and Symptoms
Sapper:	A member of the RAE, also a RAE private
SAS (R):	Special Air Service (Regiment)
Sect:	Section
SENBATT:	Senegal Battalion
SIG:	Signaller. radio operator
Sitrep:	Situation report

SGT:	Sergeant
SLR:	7.62 mm Self-loading Rifle
SNCO:	Senior Non-commissioned Officer
SOAH:	School of army health
SOP:	Standard operating procedures
SQN:	Squadron (equivalent size of Infantry Company)
SSGT:	Staff Sergeant
TAMAR (op):	Troops and Medical Aid Rwanda
TsOET:	Tests of elementary training
TP:	Troop
TPT:	Transport
TUNBATT:	Tunisian Battalion
UD:	Unlawful discharge
UN:	United Nations
UNAMIR:	United Nations Assistance Mission in Rwanda
UNCIVPOL:	United Nations Civilian Police
UNHQ:	United Nations Headquarters
UNICEF:	United Nations Children's Fund (originally called United National International Children's Emergency Fund)
UNM:	United Nations Medal
UNOMUR:	United Nations Observer Mission Uganda Rwanda
UNSC:	United Nations Security Council
UNSCR:	United Nations Security Council Resolution
VCP:	Vehicle check point
Webbing:	A series of pouches for holding ammunition and rations attached to a belt and worn around the waist
WIA:	Wounded in action
WO CATR:	Warrant Officer Caterer
WO:	Warrant Officer
ZAMBATT:	Zambian Battalion
ZERO:	To calibrate the sight and barrel of a weapon with the point of aim in order to hit targets at various ranges

"He is the raw steel whose spirit has been forged in the furnace of war from the Boer campaign and Gallipoli to the present day conflicts. It has hardened under fire in difficult situations during the desert and jungle campaigns of WW2, Korea, Borneo and Vietnam. It was then tempered under modern conflicts which have been far different, where compassion, understanding and patience are as much a part of the soldier's kitbag as his war fighting skills."

Warrant Officer Arthur Francis, CSC, OAM, ex-RSM Army

Compassion, Mateship, Courage, Initiative, Loyalty, Integrity and Trust.

These core values are the backbone of the soldier and are highlighted in the personal anecdotes and stories recounted in *Aussie Soldier*.

From World War One to the modern day conflict, Australian soldiers young and old provide an up close and personal perspective on the Army's core values and how being a soldier is more then just putting on a uniform.

With anecdotes and excerpts from diaries that have never been published, plus stories and personal perspectives from the battle grounds of Europe, the jungles of New Guinea and Vietnam, the desert sands of Iraq, the complexities of Afghanistan as well as the peace keeping missions in Rwanda, Timor and Somalia, our soldiers' honest and thoughtful accounts run the gamut of emotions.

In addition *Aussie Soldier* includes stories about the Larrikin, Close Calls in Battle, extracts of Diaries and Letters as well as a Battle Book that summarises some of Australia's most famous battles and more.

Confronting, thoughtful and with a sense of humour the collection of stories featured in *Aussie Soldier* provide an insight into the human side of a high profile and often misconstrued field of expertise.

Available at all good bookstores or purchase online at www.bigskypublishing.com.au
Postage within Australia is free. PO Box 303, Newport NSW 2106 Australia
Ph: 612 9918 2168 Fx: 612 9918 2396

Available October 2008

SOLDIERS'

A collection of true stories from Aussie Soldiers

Tales

Edited by Denny Neave

" *Plodding through mud up to the knees for days on end with a 25lb pack plus weapons and ammunition made me curse the war in no uncertain terms. Then one day I heard a soldier behind me praying, 'Dear God, help me pick up me feet, I'll put the bastards down.* "

Captain Glenn Davidson, New Guinea, WWII

A collection of stories that are entertaining, emotional and humorous, *Soldiers' Tales* is a wonderful tribute to the Aussie Digger.

From World War One to the modern day conflict, Australian soldiers share their stories and anecdotes usually saved for Anzac Day or a catch-up with mates over a cup of tea or an icy cold beer.

In their own words they provide a fascinating glimpse of the many funny and touching moments that our Diggers often hold tight to their chest. The collection of stories featured in *Soldiers' Tales* vividly provides a taste of what a soldier's life is like in both war and peace.

From the pyramids of Egypt where a pint-sized Captain used lateral thinking to gain respect, Anzac day on the porch with Banjo Patterson or a scorpion in the pants in Vietnam, their stories showcase the laconic sense of humour of the Aussie digger – that wonderful ability to get the job done with a sense of fun and a helping hand for a mate.

Soldiers' Tales is a collection of yarns to warm the heart and bring a smile to your face or a tear to the eye. A wonderful collection of stories that will delight readers of all ages and linger on well after the book has been put aside.

Available at all good bookstores or purchase online at www.bigskypublishing.com.au
Postage within Australia is free. PO Box 303, Newport NSW 2106 Australia
Ph: 612 9918 2168 Fx: 612 9918 2396

Aussie SOLDIER

HELP WITH OUR NEXT BOOK
Aussie Soldier – Iraq and Afghanistan

Are you interested in participating in the next *Aussie Soldier* book.

If you have served in either Iraq or Afghanistan and are interested in participating in the next *Aussie Soldier* book we would like to hear from you.

Register by email to **military@bigskypublishing.com.au** or by post.

Simply include your name, contact details, unit, year of deployment and a brief statement in relation to your contribution.

All contributions welcome so have your say.

General Submissions
If you believe you can help with the above projects or have a manuscript or contributions that you are interested in publishing please contact us.

Big Sky Publishing
PO Box 303
Newport NSW 2106

Email:
General   **info@bigskypublishing.com.au**
Military   **military@bigskypublishing.com.au**

Visit www.bigskypublishing.com.au for further information including other projects and books.